This book is riveting. I could not put it down. Pat and Tammy McLeod share their story of being "hit hard" by their eldest son's head injury in a high school football game. With twists and turns, their story moves from sadness to joy and back again, but always informs and provides hope. While this book is about a child who is brain injured, it will be helpful for anyone coping with losses of any kind. The awful challenge is to embrace change—especially a change we loathe. In *Hit Hard*, the McLeods share their journey of how, with faith and dignity, they are coping with loss. I recommend this book not only for professionals but also for those who want to learn how to live with loss of any kind, clear or ambiguous.

DR. PAULINE BOSS, Professor Emeritus, University of Minnesota; author of *Ambiguous Loss* and other books

A stirring and inspiring story about loss, grief, love, and faith. Pat and Tammy McLeod have much to teach us all about the meaning of ambiguous loss—how they let go of the son they once knew and learned to embrace the son they have today.

BEN BRADLEE JR., former Pulitzer Prize–winning journalist at the *Boston Globe*; author of *The Kid: The Immortal Life of Ted Williams* and *The Forgotten: How the People of One Pennsylvania County Elected Donald Trump and Changed America*

On the surface, *Hit Hard* tells the story of a young man's brain trauma and its long-term impact on the McLeod family. But there is far more to this book than a story about a catastrophic injury. Parents Pat and Tammy alternate as authors, often reflecting on the same incident from two points of view. In essence, they weave two stories into one, which underscores how each member of a family—of a community, really—is affected so differently by the same loss, especially a loss that never ends. The story itself is compelling on its own. But their honesty, their maturity of faith, their confession of hope, and their commitment to deal with the harsh reality of the experience without yielding to despair set this book apart as profound, insightful, and helpful. I was so captured that I read it in one sitting.

GERALD L. SITTSER, Professor of Theology, Whitworth University; author of *A Grace Disguised*

Hit Hard is a gripping, brutally honest narrative of the emotional devastation of parents and siblings when the athletically gifted eldest son suffers severe brain injury in a football accident, and of the disruptive effects of the injury on family relationships. When, after several years of flailing about in their grief, the family learns to identify what they are experiencing as "ambiguous loss," they are finally able to acknowledge and celebrate what is good and precious in the life of their son, especially his unbounded joy in family and friends, and his unwavering faith in God. Told by the parents in alternating sections, the story is both gut-wrenching and inspiring.

NICHOLAS WOLTERSTORFF, Noah Porter Professor of Philosophical Theology, Yale University; Senior Research Fellow, Institute for Advanced Studies in Culture, University of Virginia

The McLeod family has been on a remarkable journey. By sharing the highs, the lows, and the unvarnished truth of their son Zachary's serious brain injury, they invite us all to reflect on finding meaning in tragedy, coping with a new reality, and discovering the depth of a family's love.

CHRIS NOWINSKI, PHD, cofounder and CEO, Concussion Legacy Foundation; author of *Head Games: The Global Concussion Crisis*

One of the greatest destroyers of hope in our lives is a lack of honesty about pain, grief, and loss. In *Hit Hard*, Pat and Tammy McLeod share, with painful honesty, the reality of living through ambiguous loss together as a family. I wept several times reading this book and was moved by their commitment to Christ and especially their son Zach's focus on God. If you are experiencing loss, this book will bring you hope, comfort, joy, and a certainty that you are not alone.

MATT MIKALATOS, author of *Good News for a Change* and *Sky Lantern*

Spiritual, riveting, compassionate, loving, cathartic, and so much more. A must-read for every parent and parent-to-be.

DR. ROBERT C. CANTU, Clinical Professor of Neurosurgery and Neurology and Cofounder of the CTE Center, Boston University School of Medicine.

Hit Hard is a story of tragedy, grief, heartbreak, acceptance, hope, and redemption that will encourage every reader who has also been hit hard by the reality of this life in a fallen world outside the Garden of Eden. I have been privileged to know Pat and Tammy through this difficult journey. I have witnessed, through the pain and challenges, their struggle to accept the unknown and begin grieving without closure. Their faith has inspired me, and Zach is so fortunate to have parents who are deeply committed to Christ and to him. *Hit Hard* does not answer the question of why these difficult things happen to faithful believers. It does provide an inspirational guide to what we are to do when the challenge before us is so great that, without faith in a faithful God, we would lose our way. Pat and Tammy do not lose their way. Instead they show the rest of us how to find ours.

STEPHEN ARTERBURN, bestselling author and founder of NewLife Ministries and Women of Faith

Jesus told us that in this life we will have trouble (John 16:33). *Hit Hard* is a heartfelt and courageous testimony of fear, disillusionment, and hope in the midst of loss. Pat and Tammy corroborate the reality of so many Christians who walk through the shadow of death and still feel evil. In this regard, *Hit Hard* is a generous and empathetic love offering to the body of Christ.

JONATHAN L. WALTON, Plummer Professor of Christian Morals, Harvard University

I've known Pat and Tammy McLeod since 1986. This is the story about how their family's life changed when their sixteen-year old son, Zach, suffered a traumatic brain injury after a routine hit during a high school football game. It is a story about marriage and its imperfections; about parenting and its vulnerability; about the struggle of faith in life's uncertainty. It is a story about overwhelming grief and unexpected slivers of grace; about loneliness and friendship; about finding a marker when you are lost. It is a story about finding a name for their experience—ambiguous loss—and trying to hang on to God and each other when sometimes "hanging on" is all you can do. You will find yourself in this story somewhere. As I read it, I thought of being a parent, being a child, being a brother, being a friend, and being a person of faith. I cried and I laughed . . . it seemed like real life.

> DR. RON SANDERS, author of *After the Election* and Campus Minister at Stanford University

Hit Hard hits hard. By sharing their experience through story, Pat and Tammy offer humanity a wonderful gift from their struggle, making meaning of their loss in the crucible called life. Their story resonates with issues that transcend geographic location, class, and race, not only because it interweaves their experiences in South Africa and in the US, but because ambiguous loss and its ubiquitousness is a reality for many people across the world.

> EDWIN SMITH, former director of the University of Pretoria Mamelodi campus; cofounder of the Mamelodi Initiative; author of *Immortal: A Poetic Memento for Vuyisile Miles Smith*

Good stories can help us find meaning in the midst of devastating tragedy. *Hit Hard* is one of those stories. It's a hard but wonderful story that shows us how to deal with unimaginable loss.

> MATT CARROLL, Pulitzer Prize–winning member of the *Boston Globe*'s journalistic team whose coverage was the basis for the Oscar-winning movie *Spotlight*

This book of courage and faith in the midst of a cruel and senseless tragedy helps us make sense of what seems incomprehensible.

MICHEAL FLAHERTY, CEO of Epiphany Story Lab;
cofounder of Walden Media

Clarity. That is what this book brings to those searching for meaning in the midst of loss and suffering, or for those who feel caught up in a story that has no last chapter.

BOB SWENSON, ex All-Pro linebacker, Denver Broncos;
founder of the Freedom 58 Project

HIT HARD

One Family's Journey
of Letting Go of What Was—
and Learning to Live Well
with What Is

Pat & Tammy McLeod
with Cynthia Ruchti

TYNDALE
MOMENTUM®

The nonfiction imprint of
Tyndale House Publishers, Inc.

Visit Tyndale online at www.tyndale.com.

Visit Tyndale Momentum online at www.tyndalemomentum.com.

Visit Pat and Tammy McLeod at www.patandtammymcleod.com.

TYNDALE, *Tyndale Momentum*, and Tyndale's quill logo are registered trademarks of Tyndale House Publishers, Inc. The Tyndale Momentum logo is a trademark of Tyndale House Publishers, Inc. Tyndale Momentum is the nonfiction imprint of Tyndale House Publishers, Inc., Carol Stream, Illinois.

Hit Hard: One Family's Journey of Letting Go of What Was—and Learning to Live Well with What Is

Designed by Ron C. Kaufmann

Published in association with the literary agency of Books & Such Literary Management, 52 Mission Circle, Suite 122, PMB 170, Santa Rosa, CA 95409.

For information about special discounts for bulk purchases, please contact Tyndale House Publishers at csresponse@tyndale.com, or call 1-800-323-9400.

ISBN 978-1-4964-2533-1

Printed in the United States of America

25   24   23   22   21   20   19
7   6   5   4   3   2   1

*In times of crisis,
every relationship becomes
an at-risk relationship.*

CONTENTS

OUR STORY

    Prologue   *xiii*

    Chapters 1–19   *1*

    Photo Gallery   *226*

    Acknowledgments   *235*

    Writer's Note   *239*

RESOURCES

    Creating Your Own Ambiguous Loss
    Ritual or Ceremony   *241*

    Learning to Live with Ambiguous Loss
    and to Support Others in Theirs   *245*

    Holding On to Your Closest
    Relationship in Ambiguous Loss   *249*

    Notes from Tammy about Football
    and CTE   *251*

    Additional Resources for Your Own
    Hard Hits   *255*

    Meeting God in the Midst of Pain
    and Loss   *257*

    Resting in Scriptures for Times of Loss   *259*

    Endnotes   *263*

    About the Authors   *267*

Prologue

Pat

My wife, Tammy, and I had fallen hard for Montana in the years we lived and worked there. Everything about it stirred our senses. The mountains, wide spaces, fresh air, piercingly blue sky, and pristine lakes stretched our legs and our souls. It added to our joy that our children—a girl and three boys—appreciated the beauty and all it offered as much as we did.

After we moved to Boston, returning to Montana for vacations felt like being back home, in a place where we could look out the window and see not a bustling city, but a bald eagle soaring over a glassy lake, or the moose our son Zach nicknamed "Old Mangey" pruning the willow trees around our cabin, or the black bear that pillaged our raspberry bushes and once climbed onto our porch swing to peek in at my mom while she was in the bathroom.

Montana—even for short visits—afforded us everything we needed to thrive as a family. Togetherness. Exploration. Time and room to wander and ponder. Physical challenges that strengthened muscles and relationships. Serenity that seeped deep into our souls.

Until the day the storm hit.

Five-year-old Soren and his ten-year-old brother, Zach, had begged their grandpa to let them spend a little more time fishing from the dock while he went up to the cabin to clean fish. Tammy and I were attending a wedding. Chelsea and Nate were away with their cousins.

A Montana storm came out of nowhere, tossing a small aluminum fishing boat tethered to the dock and threatening our two sons standing nearby. The boys' grandparents were unaware of what was happening until they heard hail pinging against the roof. Then clunking on the roof. Then pounding on it.

Peering through the storm, they could barely see the dock, and no one hustling up the incline toward the cabin. All they could see and hear were a machine-gun barrage of hailstones and a sudden jarring thunderbolt.

The crisis was over by the time our family was reunited. My mom and dad, however, were still shaken. As my dad related details of the incident later, I felt every emotion, every surge of adrenaline that I would have felt if racing through the storm myself to reach my sons.

Tammy wrapped her arms around five-year-old Soren as if he were still shivering. I fist-bumped his protector, Zach, who acted as if heroism was no big deal.

"Way to go, buddy. Way to look out for your little brother."

The calm I hoped I projected didn't match my pounding heartbeat. Neither boy was seriously injured. But I knew from my own childhood that a Montana hailstorm can kill livestock.

It could have ended differently.

The boys had scrambled off the exposed dock into the boat. Soren had curled into a ball at the bottom as Zach threw life jackets over him, then hunched over his brother, shielding Soren from the pelting hail. Zach hadn't even considered his own needs in light of his brother's.

It didn't surprise any of us. It was so like Zach.

As the storm clouds on all fronts cleared, Tammy and I leaned into each other and she sighed against my chest.

"I think we should probably forgive Zach for that stunt he pulled last week with the four-wheeler," I whispered.

"Already did," Tammy said.

Holding her in that moment reminded me how blessed we were to have each other, these four unique children, and the adventure of watching them discover their place in the world.

Six years later, we were hit hard by a different storm. We weren't there to see that one strike either.

1

Tammy

"Pat, can't you drive any faster?"

"You want me to get us all killed?" Pat glanced my way.
"Sorry. I didn't mean—"

"I know."

I gripped the seat belt that lay across my chest and lifted
it away from my body so I could breathe easier. The crushing
pressure remained. The pain's genesis must have been internal.

Pat checked his rearview mirror and pressed down on the
accelerator. Boston traffic. He hit the blinker and steered our
car into the other lane, swerving in front of a slow-moving
delivery truck.

From the backseat, I heard eleven-year-old Soren draw a

sharp breath, reminding me we weren't alone in this race to the hospital. I glanced over my shoulder. Soren sat, wide-eyed, tugging at his own chest strap.

I turned to watch Boston fly past my passenger window, but Pat's profile reflected back to me in the glass. Even without a clear image, I could see the distress written all over his posture.

"Tell me again exactly what Nate said to you on the phone, Pat." As if recounting it one more time would uncover a new detail—a missing fact that would make sense of the message our fourteen-year-old son had screeched over the phone, jerking our hearts out of rhythm. I listened again as Pat repeated the scant information he had received from Nate.

I'm the no-nonsense one between us. I'm the give-it-to-me-straight person. But I'm also a ponderer. Nothing about the minutes between us and the hospital gave me anything to slide into orderly notches. Logic? Absent. Thoughts worth hovering over? Gone.

Pat's focus was still trained on the traffic in front of us, and behind us, and on either side.

Before. Behind. Beside. Familiar words in unfamiliar territory.

"We have to be prepared, Tammy," Pat whispered.

"Is Zach going to be okay?" Soren's vocal cords registered enough tension for all of us.

Sure he is lay on the tip of my tongue. *Why wouldn't Zach be okay?* I couldn't nudge the words any farther.

No matter how fast we drove or how much traffic we negotiated, the distance between us and the hospital seemed to widen rather than shrink.

We should have been at the scrimmage.

"Regret travels at the speed of light," Pat spoke into our silence.

How had he known what I was thinking? We *would* have been there. But we'd been responsible for organizing the meeting that evening where hundreds of Boston students would take their first steps toward integrating faith and college life.

Zach's scrimmage. There'd be others we could attend. Now that idea seemed absurd. We'd been laughing with, hugging, and counseling other parents' kids in our role as campus chaplains at the defining moment when, twenty miles outside of Boston, our sixteen-year-old Zach took a hard hit on a high school football field.

Now stoplights and speed limits, like referees on a field, had become impediments in the way of getting to our son.

Pat

A gut-bruising unlike any other. An excruciating pain in my chest. Though I'd played a lifetime of sports, I don't remember a hit like the one I felt when Tammy and I were finally allowed into Zach's cubicle in the Boston Medical Center trauma unit.

Zach had four faces—relentless joy, I'm-plotting-a-joke-you-don't-know-about-yet, intimate worship, and irrepressible compassion. But now it reflected no reaction. His face was expressionless. Blank. Empty of everything that defined our son.

Temporary. This is only a temporary condition. When the shock wears off . . .

I'd seen hard hits before. Came with the territory of being a football family. My grandfather played football. My dad played and coached football. Both of my brothers played football—one professionally for the Green Bay Packers. I'd played college football and coached high school football before my current job in Boston with Harvard students. We McLeods knew about hard hits.

We knew risks exist with any sport. They'd all seemed worth it. But at that moment, as I held Zach's limp hand and searched his face for the slightest flicker of life, I realized I didn't know anything at all.

I should have been there on the sidelines. Guilt came as an unbidden distraction.

While Zach was lying on the football field, Tammy and I stood with our youngest—Soren—at the back of an auditorium filled with college students. None of the hundreds of smiling, laughing, chatty students seemed in a hurry to leave when the first citywide meeting of the year ended. The walls vibrated like a stadium after a victorious homecoming football game, as if Harvard had just beaten Yale. Close friends who had spent the summer on different coasts spotted each other across the room and screamed like revelers in a mosh pit at a rock concert.

I had been caught up in the celebration and reunions until I felt a tug on my sleeve in the middle of a conversation. A Harvard student—Julia—handed me her phone. I might have been irritated by her impatience if it hadn't been for the look of anguish on her face.

I held her phone to my ear and heard panic in Nate's voice, our middle son. He was supposed to be at the meeting with us, but he'd begged to stay home that night.

"Dad, why aren't you answering your phone?" Nate's words tumbled out as if pouring through a fissure in a dam. "I've been trying to reach you. Zach's hurt." His voice hitched. "Coaches have been calling. Parents of other players are calling. Now the hospital is calling!"

Drama came second nature to Nate. I hesitated to indulge him without knowing the details.

It wasn't the first time we'd received a phone call that one of our four children had been injured. Nate had broken his arm five times. We'd deal with it. Inconvenient, but parenting is rarely convenient. In the moment, I briefly hoped whatever had happened wouldn't be serious enough to make Zach miss that week's game. He was tough. He'd played hurt before.

But I'd pressed the borrowed phone to one ear and covered the other with my hand while I made my way out of the noisy auditorium.

"He collapsed during the scrimmage," Nate said.

"Collapsed?"

"They're taking him to the hospital. In a helicopter!" His voice wavered again. "Dad, they said they need your permission to perform emergency brain surgery."

What? No. Kids get broken bones and twisted ankles. Not emergency brain surgery.

Minutes later, after I'd rounded up Tammy and Soren, we were in the car darting in and out of traffic on Massachusetts Avenue. The three of us arrived, breathless, at the door of the emergency room. We left Soren with a band of five speechless, stoic, obviously troubled football coaches so Tammy and I could get to Zach.

Now she and I stood on opposite sides of the gurney. I couldn't read what was going on in her mind. And I couldn't process what was going on in mine, much less Zach's. *Come on, buddy. Open your eyes. Say something. Say anything.*

I struggled to square the energetic young man I knew with the unmoving, unresponsive son lying in front of me.

"We're here, Zach."

Tammy's head was bowed. She rocked side to side as she had when she'd held Zach and our other children as newborns. Same Zach. *That* one.

The boy whose love for the outdoors and passion for adventure emerged during his early life in rugged Montana. The son who, nine years before, had wholeheartedly embraced urban life when we moved to Boston. The boy who'd exchanged being pulled on a horse-drawn sled for hopping on the back of a UPS truck while it raced around the streets of our Boston-Cambridge neighborhood. The one who'd replaced deer hunting with tackling our temporary rodent problem using his pellet gun, on the lookout for the rat he spotted in the basement every morning when he retrieved his bike.

That same boy now lay before us, still clad in the bottom half of his football uniform, including his football cleats. Zach's eerily unmoving body mocked the boy he'd been, the one who traded riding his bike along logging trails of a national forest for weaving in, out, and over the potholes and granite curbs of Boston. *That's my Zach.* Tough and resilient.

Zach's steady breathing slowed my pulse. Zach was *breathing.* His face was blank, but peaceful—no sign of pain.

When the surgeon burst through the doors with an entourage of doctors and nurses, he brought all the pain with him.

"We need to open his skullcap and remove a blood clot to save his life," the surgeon said, mincing no words. "This can result in anything from death to full recovery or anything in between." Handing us a clipboard, he added, "Sign here."

Chilled by the cold words and emotionless delivery, we signed. We weren't invited to ask questions but probably couldn't have thought of any after a blow like that.

A nurse broke the tense residual silence left in the surgeon's wake. "You can talk to your son. He hears you."

How does she know? Tammy and I took Zach's hands, leaned over him, and breathed in the ripe-athlete smell of our first man-child. We whispered a prayer in each ear and kissed his cheeks, our faces a much-loved son apart.

Two startling clicks announced that the nurses had unlocked the wheels of his bed. They could waste no more time.

I expected Tammy would melt into my embrace when we were left alone. I hadn't expected to feel as if I wasn't strong enough to hold myself upright, much less her. Or that instead of remaining in my embrace, she'd push away too soon and head for the waiting room to console the growing crowd of the concerned.

In the moment just before we stood alone, we watched the medical staff steer Zach through the double door toward a surgery with the power to give his life back . . . or take it from him.

∞

I watched Coach Papas—the weight on his shoulders palpable—as I headed toward him and a group of empty chairs in the corner of the waiting room. This was not a man known for his softness—at least, on the football field. He was as intense and demanding as they come. If a player arrived for practice on time, Coach Papas considered him ten minutes late. The man elicited respect bordering on fear from his football players, including Zach.

I reached to shake his hand before asking the unanswerable question. "Coach, what happened? I don't understand."

The coach with a reputation for toughness dissolved in tears and tried to recount what had transpired.

On the first play of the game, Zach intercepted a pass and ran it back for a touchdown. Then—an unremarkable play. Zach and four other teammates tackled a running back. Nothing out of the ordinary. Zach went down with the pile, but it wasn't clear if his helmet hit another player's. He stumbled on the way back to the huddle. Unusual, but not worrisome. The coach made a joke about Zach tripping over the paint on the yard line, brought him in to discuss the next play, and looked into his eyes.

That's when Coach Papas knew something was wrong.

"I'm fine, Coach," Zach had said with his signature enthusiasm.

And then he collapsed at the coach's feet.

"I've seen lots of my players go down," Coach Papas said. "Nothing like this." His words trailed off, disappearing into the swirl of conversations, the endless echo—*How could this have happened?*

As Coach Papas finished sketching the details of what led to this moment, other friends and family members poured into the quickly shrinking space in the waiting room.

Tammy and I fielded a steady stream of questions. Our answers consisted largely of "We don't know" or "We don't know yet." I caught glimpses of Tammy moving from one person to another, offering comfort.

Tammy's strength didn't surprise me. It warmed me in the air-conditioned chill of the waiting room. She saw a need and, as she usually did, stepped up to meet it. She tamed what must have been her own raging internal upheaval to serve those locked in confusion and concern. I admired that pattern in her and had seen it often. For some reason, on this night, my admiration was tinged with—*what?*—loneliness?

We'd always worked well together—as a couple, as parents, as partners in serving the spiritual needs of college students. Still tag-teaming, we operated in our strengths—Tammy calming others, me capturing all the details I could. Only a few feet apart from each other. She turned a pained smile my way.

Suffocating numbness enshrouded me. Emotional asthma. I couldn't exhale. Couldn't inhale. Out of sight, away from our presence, doctors huddled over our son, attempting to use all of medicine's resources and their well-honed skills to preserve Zach's scrambled brain, to save his life.

How could a cohesive, rational thought push past that reality?

Tammy

So many people. Our circle of friends was large, diverse, younger, older . . . what a gift. We'd never be able to thank them all. I made my rounds, giving and receiving hugs, thanking them for coming, as if they'd taken off work to attend a funeral.

"Thank you for coming."

"Thank you for coming."

"Thank you for coming."

Their presence was a comfort, but it also underscored the seriousness of our unfolding family drama.

2

Pat

As we waited, my mind drifted to South Africa and scenes from our summer trip. I saw Zach leaning over an industrial-sized sink as he scrubbed pots and pans. He pulled a soapy soup ladle out of the water and belted out the first line of a South African folk song to the hoots and hollers of the kitchen staff who had taught him the words.

I'd walked in on that moment just a month before Zach's injury. Our family had taken a team of twenty-five students—most from Harvard and Stanford—to South Africa on a service learning project. We'd cared for children orphaned by HIV/AIDS, as well as children with severe physical and mental disabilities.

Now I sat a world away in a hospital waiting room next to Anne, a good friend from the school community who had slipped into the chair beside me.

"How are you doing, Pat?"

"I'm . . . hanging in there."

Anne's unruffled voice and conversation attempts floated out of reach until she asked me to talk about the South African trip already on my mind. A diversionary tactic? It worked. The country held so much of Zach's heart. Talking about it with Anne let me escape the current circumstances and relive the exceptional experience of serving as a family.

The scene in the kitchen had actually followed a few days of conflict between Zach and me. Our team spent our days working with the kids. Zach had rarely been free of two or three of the children climbing on him, teasing him, delighting in his impromptu comedy routines, guitar playing, or soccer scrimmages. But my joy at seeing how effortlessly he toggled between our world and theirs morphed into irritation when I noticed he was arriving late to our post-dinner training sessions.

One evening I watched Zach sneak into the room where the team met to regroup and plan for the next day. He ducked his head and took a seat in the back row. I clenched my jaw. *Late for the third straight night.* Here I was, leading a discussion on teamwork, and my own son couldn't bother to show up on time.

When the meeting ended, I walked over to him as he joked with several college students. I stood back a few feet and waited for them to finish.

"Zach, what's going on?" I finally asked when the other

guys drifted away. "You can't continue showing up late to these sessions."

He shrugged and smiled.

Irritation rose in my chest. "You're not taking these meetings seriously, Zach! I don't appreciate your casual attitude. I want you here on time! Got it?"

My question forced his hand. He reluctantly confessed that he had been sneaking into the kitchen after our meals and taking over the job of washing our dishes instead of letting the South African kitchen staff clean up after us. He wanted to serve. He knew enough about the history of systemic racism in South Africa and America to object to the idea of expecting them to serve him.

When pressed, he said he'd done it secretly because he didn't want to make a big deal about it or draw attention to himself or make others feel obligated to serve with him.

Eventually someone on our team figured out what Zach had been up to and joined him. One by one, others followed. Where others in high positions had struggled to smooth race relations, Zach had come up with his own solution—Americans cleaning up their own messes in exchange for the kitchen staff singing to them their favorite African worship songs.

"I imagine you had many unforgettable moments over there," Anne said.

"Many," I said. I paused for a breath. It came easier than it had moments before.

"I had to hide my shock when we first entered the children's home. The severely disfigured bodies, the occasional piercing cries or unsettling moans of some of the kids, and the nauseating stench that lingered in the air . . ."

I remarked to Anne about the satisfaction I'd felt in the orphanage one day as I looked around and realized our students were learning their largest life lessons from kids who couldn't read and had no opportunity for formal schooling much less a college education, children who in some cases struggled to manage the basic functions of their bodies.

"None of us expected that working with children with disabilities would become the highlight of the summer," I told Anne.

I caught Tammy's glance from across the room. As in South Africa, we were in this together. As always.

Revisiting Africa was much preferred to concentrating on the reason our orbits had been relocated to a hospital. "By the end of the project," I told Anne, "Zach's little rebellion—and our invitation for the kitchen staff to stay, as long as they agreed to sing for us—transformed a kitchen into a sanctuary, a group of independent individuals into a community, and the messy, mundane work of washing dishes into worship."

"I love it when a sixteen-year-old kid leads the way," Anne said.

Tammy's orbit brought her close to the conversation. Close enough to add, "While we were in South Africa, several of the college girls on our team teasingly asked us for Zach's hand in marriage, or mourned that he wasn't a few years older."

I caught Tammy's hand in mine, grateful to be tethered to her. "Most of them rescinded their offers on the next-to-last day of the trip."

"You don't have to tell *that* story," Tammy said, easing her hand free and nudging my shoulder.

How do I express this to Anne? "Zach filled a paper bag with baboon droppings, put it on the girls' front porch, and lit the bag on fire. When the girls came out of the door screaming and stomped out the fire, they—"

"I get the picture," Anne said, laughing.

As our smiles faded, an unexpected calm settled over me. Moments ago, I had mentally been in South Africa, reliving a remarkable season of joy. I'd blinked and found myself back in a Boston hospital. Anne's ploy had worked. It wasn't that her perceptive questions tricked me into denying the seriousness of the present crisis. Rather, she was the first to help me connect the overwhelming tragedy of our present crisis to a larger story.

I let a flicker of hope and consolation wash over me. This ordeal wasn't the whole story. Zach's chapter—however long or short—was part of the larger story God has been unveiling to humanity since the beginning of time.

I looked up to find Tammy. She was praying with one of the comforters. Sharing the glimmer of hope would have to wait.

Tammy

Two a.m.

The hospital staff informed us that the surgery was finished, and we could soon join Zach in the intensive care unit. We said good night to the coach and all but one of Pat's closest friends, Marty, who insisted he would stay the night with Pat in the hospital. Marty suggested I go home and sleep after we'd had a chance to see our son and talk to the doctor.

We'd met the brain surgeon only briefly before Zach was whisked away. I both appreciated and hated that the surgeon had wasted no energy on excess words. I've always appreciated those who cut through the small talk and get to the point. But at two in the morning, after the tension of waiting through four hours of surgery, I found myself longing for more than his quick sentences: "We did what we had to do. We stopped the bleeding. We removed the blood clot. Now we have to wait."

With an expressionless nod of his head, he dismissed himself.

Nurses filled in the blanks—and there were many—explaining that Zach would remain in a medically induced coma for the next several days while the medical team sought to manage the brain swelling.

The brain, they told us, is prone to swell for at least five days after Zach's kind of injury. If that couldn't be kept under control, the surgeons would have to open him up again. They'd remove his skullcap for an extended period of time to give his brain space to expand and recover.

"But you want to make sure you get a second opinion before doing that," Zach's male nurse warned us, "because I've never seen anyone fully recover from that surgery."

Razor-edged, scalpel-edged words. I pushed aside the visual of my son without the top of his skull, the skeletal helmet divinely designed to protect the human brain.

Most mothers are taught to guard a baby's fontanel, his or her soft spot, since the bones need time to close to protect a newborn's brain development. I had gently stroked the spot on each of my children while I sang over them.

I'd rocked this child—Zach—in silence in the middle of the night while a Montana moon rose over the mountains. With a canopy of a million stars watching, I'd stroked his cheek and kissed his sweet-smelling head, that very spot.

How elusive such serenity seemed in the dark hospital room.

Hours earlier, Pat and I had had only questions. Now at least we had one answer. Would Zach survive the surgery? Yes. But would he emerge from this crisis whole, half, or not at all? Too soon to tell.

Who can describe what it's like to send their son off to school in the morning and before the next dawn walk into a hospital room with that boy unconscious, bandaged, hooked to machines measuring respiration, blood pressure, heartbeats, and intercranial pressure? Wires and tubing and the gurgling of the oxygen machine filled the space. Hand in hand, Pat and I had walked in on a scene from a medical drama. *Our* drama.

My son lay absolutely still in front of me. I'd had no choice in the decision to keep him in a comatose state. If asked, I would have begged for a few moments with him first. A minute. One. Long enough to tell him I loved him. Long enough to hear him call me "Peach" one more time. His nickname for me—adopted from what Pat had occasionally called me—had always warmed me.

I leaned over my no-longer-an-infant son and flinched at the sight of the head I'd kissed during those sacred midnight feedings.

Thick, bulky bandages surrounded a protruding bolt that measured his intercranial pressure. He was intubated, so I couldn't touch his lips. His feet were ensconced in puffy Frankenstein-like boots to assist blood flow back to the heart and prevent clots. I wanted to hold my son. To touch my son's sweet head. My hand lifted unbidden, then fell empty to the bedside.

Open your eyes, Zach. Look at me. Tell me you're going to be okay.

Pat

As much as I loved Tammy, it was hard to look her in the eye after Zach's surgery. The pain contorting her face tore at me. Stress is a fickle glue. Our concern over Zach should have cemented us to each other. Instead, we drew our agony around ourselves like a force field. Inadequate protection at best. Distance-maker at worst. It was as if letting ourselves be vulnerable with each other would have made us brittle. We couldn't afford to crumble.

We barely spoke about our concerns unless we were alone, as if afraid that if Zach's subconscious heard our fears, he might be rattled. We knew our son. His compassion for people— including his parents—might spike his blood pressure or cause his pulse to race. Neither would aid his healing. So we did little talking in Zach's presence, other than to encourage his still form with words that sounded too much like a pregame pep talk.

Tammy

Chelsea. I kept thinking about her as I drove home alone from the hospital. The oldest of our children, Chelsea had left home two weeks before. She was independent, more than ready to make her way in the world as a freshman in college. But the first year comes with built-in anxieties. And now she was halfway across the country, working her way through all the newness of college life, dorm mates, and endless decisions.

Why didn't we call her as soon as they rolled Zach into the operating room?

Pat had wanted to spare Chelsea. "She's a thousand miles away," he'd said when we sat in the hospital waiting room.

"We'll call her when we have something to report. What do we know for sure yet? Nothing. Let's at least wait until he gets out of surgery. Why worry her if this is a simple fix?"

It hadn't been simple. A four-hour brain surgery. And by the time it was over, we would have had to wake her in the middle of the night. How was she going to handle the news that her best friend and brother had undergone brain surgery and was on a respirator in a medically induced coma? She shouldn't have to deal with this. No one should.

It was too late to call her now. I'd do that first thing in the morning.

My mind jumped from Chelsea to Nate and Soren. All of my energy had been focused solely on Zach; but now, in the quiet of the predawn hours, the weight of how this was affecting his brothers was heavy on my shoulders.

I arrived at the house and let myself into our second-floor apartment at the Wilson House, a 118-year-old Victorian—our home for the past nine years, a church-owned residence we shared with campus ministers. The structure is massive, with a separate entrance for us.

Home felt hollow with no one there. A friend had graciously offered Soren and Nate her guest room for the night. I stumbled through the hallway as if I were the one wearing Frankenstein boots. Now I stood outside Nate's bedroom, imagining how terrified he had been when he desperately tried to reach us. *Nate, oh Nate.* He'd borne the gravity of Zach's condition longer than any of us. *God, heal him. Heal us all.*

My eyes burned. Sleep. I needed sleep.

Pat needed sleep, too, but he'd said he couldn't imagine leaving Zach's side. I appreciated Pat's devotion, but our son wasn't going to suddenly sit up and start talking as if nothing had happened. This was no joke, no prank. The heavy doses of medication meant Zach wouldn't wake until the doctors decided it was safe for his brain to emerge from its protective coma.

Our oldest son was gone, for a while. Not forever. The faintest whisper said, "Maybe forever?" No. I wouldn't entertain that thought.

How does a person manage a loss that isn't?

Zach's door was ajar.

I nudged it open with my foot. He hadn't made his bed. A messy bed wouldn't be an issue for him for a while. Someone in hospital scrubs would tend to that task until he was well enough. Zach would find it ironic that he'd finally discovered a way out of that despised chore.

The neck of his guitar rested on his pillow, the body of the instrument where Zach should be. The strings silent. Its soundboard scratched from a million teenaged strums. If I closed my eyes, I could almost see his long fingers forming the chords, hear the music, catch his voice lifted in worship.

You give and take away. You give and take away. . . . Lord, blessed be your name. *

No. Not that song. I could embrace only part of those lyrics. God gives. He *gives*.

I closed the door behind me in search of my own pillow.

---

*Here and following, source information for quotations is available in the endnotes section in the back of the book.

CHAPTER

3

Pat

Nearly two days of mind-numbing sameness had passed since the surgery without the miraculous awakening for which we—and the whole community—prayed. Zach's brain pressures fell, then rose, then fell, then rose, like a tenacious New England winter unwilling to give in to spring. Tammy and I could watch the monitor, and the nurses taught us what it meant. The medical team reported no signs of anything resembling steady forward progress.

I finally slept, drifting off in the chair that converted into a temporary bed in Zach's room.

Exhaustion forced me to sleep. But it was restless sleep couched in a disturbing dream. An ancient, familiar story.

Abraham and Isaac, walking side by side up the mountain to worship. Every step took Abraham closer to the horrifying reality that obedience meant being willing to offer his son as a sacrifice.

Abraham and Isaac disappeared from my dream, and suddenly I was standing on the mountain with my firstborn son. Zach was whole, full of life. But there was no last-minute pardon like the one Abraham received.

I woke, screaming, "No! I can't let you have him!"

Someone touched my arm. "Are you okay, Mr. McLeod?"

I looked up into the concerned face of the night nurse, scrubbed at my eyes, and cleared my throat. "I . . . I was dreaming."

My heart continued to pound long after the nurse left. It wasn't a dream. It was a nightmare.

God, don't ask that of me. You can't ask me to give up my son. You wouldn't, would You? He's coming back. Zach's coming back to us.

A deep, murky fog replaced the dream. Would my son return unscathed from the mountain? Would he return as the bright, kind, servant-hearted young man he'd been before the injury?

Would he pull pranks and torment his siblings and bring joy to his mother's heart through their shared love of music? Would he walk right back into his passion for sports?

Would he walk?

Please bring him back the way he was before.

I glanced at the wall clock with its illuminated day and date. With dawn still too far away, it struck me that the date was significant.

It's his birthday, God. Zach's seventeenth birthday. A great day for a bleating ram to emerge from a thornbush and climb up on the altar, releasing my son.

∞

Tammy was back early in the morning. She'd probably taken care of dozens of details already. Now she fussed with the blanket at the foot of Zach's hospital bed, as if his feet could register hot and cold, or her touch.

"He's still with us." I laid my hand on Tammy's forearm. Had I said it for her or for me?

For us.

"Is he?" Tammy asked. "Do you know that for sure? What if he's not?"

Her words stung. I wanted to dwell in optimism, in the hope that all of this was temporary.

She moved toward the door.

"Where are you going?"

She turned toward me, her gaze falling somewhere over my shoulder. "People out there are waiting for an update."

Unbidden frustration expanded inside me like an airbed inflating from flat to full-sized. It pressed against my lungs. "We don't have anything to tell them. It won't hurt them to wait, Tammy."

"This room is claustrophobic. I don't know how you can stand to be in here all the time without a break, Pat."

"I don't need a break. I need to be with my son."

"*Our* son."

"That's what I meant." As soon as Zach recovered, we'd have to work on getting back onto the same page. "I appreciate all the people who are out there, too, but—"

"Our friends from church? Our students? Neighbors? Coaches? Zach's classmates? The people who have dropped everything normal in their lives to be with us because our life is anything but normal right now? They're keeping me upright through all this."

"I don't understand, Tammy. I just need to be here with Zach. You need to be with *them*. Can you explain that to me?"

"Can you explain—?" Her voice halted, as if she knew the futility of questioning our different ways of dealing with what had happened. The loss. Our loss. The loss of us, our family, any shred of what life once looked like. Lost. Temporarily or permanently? Only God knew. Nothing I could say would wipe away the pain for either of us.

My heart rhythm hiccupped. A stark reminder of what I'd almost forgotten. God knew.

"Tammy, seventeen years ago today, we chose the name Zach for a reason. Zach, Zachary—*the Lord remembers*. No matter what, the Zach we know and love can never be lost to the God who remembers."

∽

By the evening of the next day, the pressure in Zach's brain had decreased enough to call it a positive trend. The medical staff encouraged us to go home, shower, eat one of the many meals stocked in our refrigerator and freezer by caring members of Zach's school community, hug our other kids, and get a solid night's rest.

Neither of us objected to the idea, although I hesitated to leave Zach alone. Tammy convinced me they wouldn't suggest we leave if he wasn't doing okay.

Hope had some breathing room.

Marty accompanied us home and tended to odd jobs that would have been simple for us under ordinary circumstances but seemed crushing now. He became a buffer zone when natural tensions escalated between Tammy and me, and fielded questions from some of the college staff living in the first-floor apartment of the home. We were grateful for their presence, always one or more of them available to make sure the boys were okay and had what they needed, ready to step in if we were delayed at work. Or now, delayed at the hospital.

I don't know what we would have done in those early days without Marty. He'd been there for so many significant moments in my life, through two family moves, and now he was here to do whatever was necessary.

We called Chelsea, eager to pass on good news for a change, but she didn't pick up. I left a message on her voice mail. We had talked only once since the accident. Chelsea had attempted to remain calm on the phone, but her voice wavered and cracked. Her question cut deep: Why hadn't we called her immediately, right after hanging up with Nate the night of the injury? Zach's grandparents and other family members also expressed their distress at not being phoned quickly.

Conversations in the house were anything but normal. Zach's crisis had absorbed all of us into its vortex.

When we sat down for our first family dinner in days, reconnection carried an awkward undertone.

"Soren, I heard you got in trouble at school today." It had to be addressed.

Soren stopped chewing and looked me in the eye.

"You want to talk about it?" I asked.

He swallowed, looked down at his plate, and mumbled, "Why did you send me to a new school?"

Nate came to his brother's rescue. "Dad, I know Zach needs you, but so do we, and so does Mom."

Tammy glanced my way.

An unprecedented silence settled over our dinner table. A silence that wouldn't have been tolerated by Chelsea's witty sarcasm or Zach's playful storytelling. The silence signaled a sea change within our family. Everything felt different.

"Listen, I don't know how long it's going to be until things get back to normal," I told them, "but I do know one thing more than I have ever known it before—how important both of you are to me. You know that, right? Zach is down for a while, and we are all going to have to rally around to help him until our family gets back to normal."

How long would this temporary bandage cover Soren's and Nate's unseen wounds?

We made a concerted effort to catch up with extended-family emails and phone messages and checked in again with our backup team at Harvard. They'd been more understanding than we could have imagined about our need to be with Zach and had filled in all the gaps we were leaving during the most crucial days of the new school year.

We went through the motions at home. But when the adrenaline on which we'd been depending dissipated, exhaustion hit. Tammy and I crawled into beds in separate rooms to allow ourselves the best chance at our first real sleep since the trauma had begun.

Sleep was short-lived.

I dreamed that Zach's condition worsened and that the

doctors were trying to reach us by phone but couldn't wake either of us. The nightmare broke through with such overwhelming force that I woke in a cold, panicked sweat.

But I wasn't dreaming.

A voice blared from our landline's answering machine in the kitchen. One of Zach's nurses. I lunged out of bed and scrambled to the phone.

Has something awful happened? Why didn't the staff call our cell phones?

I grabbed the receiver, interrupting the caller on the other end. "This is Pat McLeod. Could you repeat what you just said?"

"Mr. McLeod, I tried to reach you and your wife on your cell phones first, but neither of you picked up. Through the night, Zach's brain began swelling uncontrollably. The surgeon is on his way to the hospital. Zach is being prepped for emergency surgery to remove part of his skull and allow room for the swelling."

Zach was still alive. I exhaled in relief. Then a rogue wave of fear crashed over me. Hadn't one of the nurses told us that first night that this kind of operation would almost certainly rule out the possibility of a full recovery?

"We'll be there as quickly as we can."

I woke Tammy—who berated herself for falling asleep at all—and opened the door of the guest room to wake Marty. Within seconds, the three of us were out the door, in the car, and speeding down the streets of the now sleeping city.

Marty noted every red light I ran. I didn't apologize. Or slow down. Not this time.

I brought the car to a screeching halt at the hospital entrance and tossed the keys to Marty. He'd find a place to park while

Tammy and I rushed to be with Zach. But Zach's ICU room was empty. They'd already taken him to the operating room.

A team of doctors waited in the hallway for our consent. The chief surgeon explained, "Your son's kidneys can no longer tolerate the high dosages of medication needed to control the brain swelling. Our only option is to remove a portion of Zach's skullcap and surgically place it in a subcutaneous pouch in his abdomen to keep the bone viable until the brain swelling stops. If all goes well, we'll eventually perform another surgical procedure to remove the section of bone from his abdomen and reattach it to his skull."

"Could we get a second opinion?" My response was prompted by the male nurse's words—that he'd never seen anyone fully recover from that procedure.

The brain surgeon paused, looked at his team, and said, "There are five other doctors here. You can ask them."

Somber and grim, they nodded in unison.

Tammy and I reluctantly signed the document authorizing the surgery. She found a quiet place to phone two of the college staff members on the first floor of the Wilson House and tell them what had happened so they could let Nate and Soren know. She informed family and friends, requesting more prayer support.

I did what came instinctively in that moment of defeat. I ran from the scene with an irrepressible need to be alone.

People weren't my answer. I wandered the maze of corridors that connected the many buildings of the hospital until I found a dark, empty waiting room where no one could find me.

But someone did. I heard him approach before I saw him.

"I know you're trying to avoid me."

Marty's hulking frame filled the doorway. "Yesterday," he said, stepping into the room, "I found a little diner across the street that opens early and serves a pretty good breakfast. Let's go get something to eat."

I didn't want to eat. I wanted to be alone in my pain. But long ago I'd learned to trust Marty's wisdom and friendship.

With the diner that close to the hospital, I suspected this was neither the first nor the last time servers would see a grown man sob over his Greek omelet. I felt like I was in the middle of a slow-motion shipwreck. The ship was sinking, and no one could change that. I could barely tread water in the swirling, debris-ridden sea of emotions—fighting to keep my nose above the waves, struggling for each breath.

Marty's steadying presence made the space around us safe enough for me to bare my heart.

"I should never have left Zach alone." I laid my fork beside my plate, the clink of metal on the tabletop a curiously rude sound in that moment. "What if he dies, Marty? Is that how this will end? What would that do to us as a family?"

"Don't borrow trouble, Pat. We have every confidence Zach will come through the surgery." He pointed to my fork.

I picked it up again but could do little more than push bits of omelet in a random pattern on the plate. "I don't know if I can be strong enough for all of them anymore."

My children stood in an imaginary line in my mind. Chelsea, her arms loaded with textbooks but with panic in her eyes. Nate, still reeling from having to be the one to tell us the news but pretending to be tougher and older than he was. Soren, lost without his big brother.

One of my children—Zach—wasn't standing.

"I'm scared, Marty."

He silently listened. As he always had. Then he caught the attention of our server and ordered a diet cola.

"Are you kidding me? You have to stop drinking that stuff," I jokingly chided. "And if you haven't noticed, it's five o'clock in the morning."

Marty raised his eyebrows but said nothing. His drink arrived moments later.

"You know what my biggest fear is . . . more than any other?" I said. "That Zach survives, but his personality is different. I don't want him to be anyone other than himself. I can't bear that thought." My voice trailed off in a hoarse whisper.

Marty took a sip of his drink and dusted breakfast crumbs from his graying beard. Then my wise friend and mentor said, "I definitely hope Zach fully recovers. But if I had to guess, I would guess he probably won't."

My throat constricted.

Then he tossed me a life preserver. "And yet I have a feeling that somehow Zach will become more delightful than ever to you."

Tammy

I couldn't bear to ask where Pat had been after he returned to the waiting room. But he smelled a little like garlic and feta, and the stricken look had vanished from his eyes. Marty joined the swelling circle of friends who now threatened to clog the hallways as well as the room where we sat.

After the surgery, Zach's abdomen sported a bulge the size and shape of a small, upside-down cereal bowl, the outline of the skullcap inside. Hope for beginning the process to ease Zach out of the medically induced coma was pushed back. Any healing that had begun in the days since his first surgery had now been erased. My grief felt like a sourdough starter that doubled in size every few minutes.

By midafternoon, Zach's vitals had stabilized enough for me to tell Pat, "I'm going for a run."

Pat's facial expression shifted. "That's what you need right now?"

"That's what I need."

"Okay."

"I'll stop at the house and check on the boys before I come back. Can I bring you anything?"

I watched my husband fight to maintain control of his emotions. Of the two of us, he'd always been the more poetic. It showed now in his expression. Lips tight, he shook his head. Like me, he apparently couldn't think of anything from home that would make any difference.

When I walked out of the hospital on my way to the running path, the bright sunlight soothed me. To others, it might have seemed a searing light underscoring the contrast between the beautiful outdoors and the reality of what was happening inside the hospital. My son, my kindred spirit, my Zach, had been mauled by a hard hit and taken from us. Maybe only temporarily. No one knew.

But the sun didn't sear. Instead its warmth enveloped me, as if it were coming at me from all sides, wrapping me rather than burning. I welcomed it. I filled my lungs with fresh air that was free of the smell of antiseptic, bleached linens, and the hospital cafeteria's burnt coffee.

As I ran—because I could—Zach lay brain-bruised and broken on the sidelines of life. My feet slapped the dirt path along the Charles River, picking up the pace. The early autumn rays lit the path ahead of me.

God, You know how much I miss him. And how grateful I am for Your nearness right now. This is hard, so hard.

I ran and prayed and cried and relived tender moments with Zach.

My son had been sidelined. Then, while still in a coma, unable to move out of the way, he'd been hit by a semi called surgery that swerved from the other lane and flattened him, ripping a chunk from his skull, tossing it aside, exposing the brain that could no longer fit in its housing. Now he was more vulnerable than he'd ever been, more vulnerable than a human should ever have to be.

Left, right, left, right shouldn't take conscious thought. I ran to regain my rhythm. When I stumbled over twigs or crunched dried leaves underfoot, I almost recoiled at having crushed them. There was entirely too much crushing going on in our lives right now.

I focused on the left-right pattern until it slid back into a recognizable beat.

Oxygen. That's what I've needed. As my lungs filled, I noticed details that had grown foggy. The smell of sun-baked leaves. Reflections that danced on the surface of the river beside the path as they had since the river first ran.

Zach's story wasn't over. It couldn't be.

This was a chapter, not a book. We'd turn the page and discover a new scene, with the nightmare over and a comforting resolution waiting on the fresh pages, like the resolution of a dissonant chord at the end of Zach's favorite worship song that played in my ears as I ran.

Behold, I am doing a new thing.

The Voice I'd been waiting to hear was speaking. Familiar words from the book of Isaiah.

I would run until it made sense. No. I couldn't wait until it made sense. Too many people needed me.

Including Pat.

Oxygen. That's what the two of us need. And You, God.

∞

I was drained yet invigorated from my run when I got to the house. It usually vibrated with people and activity. Sometimes as many as a dozen or more recent college grads occupied the other floors of the spacious residence. When life was ordinary, I fed on the flow of people, conversations, and opportunities to pour into young lives. Their vibrancy filled my soul. And Zach had been part of it, endearing himself to everyone who walked through the doors.

Today I closed the front door quietly, grateful for the un-expected silence as I gathered our mail. Among the mail and packages sat a tall cardboard box that came up to my chest. The address label read *TO: Zach McLeod.* The trembling in my legs was from the exercise after too many days of inactivity. Wasn't it?

What had he ordered? The packing tape pulled free too easily.

A new guitar.

One he would probably never play.

In a time of grief, it's the symbols that cut deepest—the single red shoe in a pile of dusty gray war rubble, the grease-stained recipe card in Grandma's handwriting, the flag-draped casket saluted at the airport, the first wildflower that pushes its way through the ashes of last year's forest fire, the guitar whose voice would never be heard.

Grief. I'd used the word *grief*. Was I pre-grieving a permanent loss that was real but not yet announced? Was I courageously bracing myself for the inevitable? What did I have to mourn? Zach wasn't lying on a marble slab in a morgue. He was in a hospital bed. Still "with us."

But the word *grief* refused to be erased from the whiteboard of my mind.

CHAPTER

4

Pat

I stood beside Zach's bed, stiff from another long day in the hospital bed-chair. My old football injuries weren't responding well to my temporary sleeping accommodations in his room. Five days in and there had been no measurable change in Zach's condition. The medical staff once again encouraged Tammy and me to go home and try to get some sleep.

But what if he wakes up? The thought made me hesitate. We had been assured that our presence could make a big difference. A patient waking from a traumatic brain injury and heavy sedation often is disoriented and starts thrashing around, the staff had warned us. Familiar voices and faces help temper the reaction.

When that time came—if it came at all—Tammy and I would need all the physical and emotional reserves we could muster to make it through. Now was the time to build our reserves, not use them up, the staff insisted.

Despite the logic of reserving our strength for when Zach would really need us, I still hesitated to leave. The last time we'd obeyed doctors' orders, our sleep had been interrupted by news of that second emergency brain surgery. But my eyes burned. My body was functioning on fumes that wouldn't get me far. Clear thinking—rarely an issue before—eluded me.

Tammy waited at the door for me. As I leaned over the bed's guardrail to kiss Zach good-bye for the night, I had to remind myself that what had happened to him during the scrimmage was a fluke. The benefits of sports far outweigh the risks.

There was a time when Tammy agreed with me on that point.

The trip home started with the two of us sorting out details for the upcoming week. Who would stay with Soren and Nate for the next few days when we were at the hospital? Who would host our weekly meeting with the Harvard student leadership team? What could we do to communicate updates about Zach more quickly and efficiently?

Then stark silence settled over us. I thought about turning on the radio to break the awkwardness. Music always brought Tammy comfort. Zach's favorite songs, the ones they shared, connected them in a love language I didn't relate to, although I sensed its incredible power. Though a classically trained musician, Tammy encouraged Zach's interest in a unique combo of jazz, rock, and worship music. But music didn't seem appropriate at the moment. Truth be told, nothing did.

At home, we walked through our routines on autopilot. Paying bills. Eating a meal whether we were hungry or not. Work-related business needed our attention, even if all we could manage were apologies for delays and abbreviated responses. Marty had gone home and was now an hour away in New Hampshire. He would have come if we'd asked, but he'd done so much already.

Time alone together bowed to the needs of the crisis. How long could that go on? We'd been thrust into an unwanted game of tug-of-soul.

I was sitting at the kitchen table finishing up an overdue project when I heard muffled sounds from Zach's bedroom. I found Tammy sitting on the floor beside our son's bed, where she often knelt and prayed with him. Now she was quietly sobbing. Zach's backpack lay open on the floor beside her.

"Honey, what are you doing?"

"Reading Zach's last journal entries. The school finally found his backpack."

"I see that."

She shifted positions. "I had to know what Zach was thinking, what was going on in his head in the days before his injury. What was he reading in his Bible? What was he writing in his journal? Had he drawn any new sketches?"

Before me was a heartbroken mother longing for a word from the son who could no longer speak. My wife. My son.

"Pat, other parents who've lost a child suddenly—" She drew a breath. "I've read of parents who took such comfort from what they'd found in their son's or daughter's journal, what they'd written, what they'd been thinking. I needed to know what Zach was thinking."

I joined her on the floor and held my wife as she read aloud from what she'd discovered among Zach's journal entries. We cried together, Tammy leaning into my grief and I into hers.

Eventually, she laid the journal in her lap. "I miss Zach."

"I do too." I held her tighter. "But—"

Tammy flinched against my embrace. "Please . . . don't say something positive to make me feel better. Just sit with me in my pain."

I didn't try to hide my weeping from her.

"Thank you," she whispered against my chest.

Until that moment, I had assumed my job—my role in the crisis—was to absorb the grief, anger, and pain building up and spilling out around Tammy and our kids. Absorb their grief so they wouldn't feel the full brunt. My job. But that night, I expressed my sorrow rather than trying to deflect or divert the hard hit Tammy had also taken. Judging from her response, it appeared more meaningful to her than the strength I'd been trying to project.

The two of us moved slowly around Zach's room, pausing in front of drawings he had sketched on the wall and reading aloud the hand-lettered Bible verses above his desk. We'd let him do what he wanted with the walls. Now, seeing his heart on display, I was grateful we hadn't painted over it.

The verses captured not only the grasp Zach had on the extent of God's love for him, but also his longing to see others come to know and experience that same love.

"This is who Zach is," I said.

Tammy laid one hand over her heart. "I don't know what verb to use."

"What?"

"*Is* or *was*? This is who Zach was? Is? Neither seems to fit."

The verb tense. Our pain had been reduced to a verb tense.

The vulnerability of the moment fed my courage to risk asking the question I hadn't yet found a way to broach.

"Tammy, have you ever thought that somehow Zach might have known this was coming?"

The evidence was all around us. Over the past months, Zach's faith had deepened to a level that moved us and at the same time made this undefinable loss all the more devastating.

Tammy's mingled tears and silence hinted that she'd wondered the same thing.

We sat on the floor next to each other again. "Zach and I had a bizarre conversation at the breakfast table a few days before he was injured," I said. "It didn't seem so . . . significant . . . at the time. I don't know why I didn't think to tell you about it until now." I looked at Tammy for assurance it was safe to continue.

Tammy leaned forward. "What conversation?"

I swallowed hard. "We were reliving our time in South Africa. Laughing. Joking. Remembering the quirky phrases and antics of the children we'd grown to love—children with special needs."

"His favorites."

"The children with disabilities." How I managed to speak that word—*disabilities*—I don't know. It tasted sour on my tongue, despite our family's strong connection to those children.

I took Tammy's hand. "Zach switched off his comedy routine that morning and said, 'This may sound weird, Dad, but I wonder if God would ever have me become like one of them.'"

"Pat!" Tammy melted against me. "What did you tell him?"

"I'm surprised I took his question seriously. But I did. And he was obviously serious."

Tammy waited.

"So I said, 'Well, Zach, you can be sure that if anything ever happened to you, if you . . . if you became disabled, we would love you the same way we love them.'"

Tammy's tears flowed for a new reason.

She pressed for more details, but there was nothing to add. I knew the time wasn't right to tell Tammy how I felt about it now, but reliving that early morning conversation with Zach marked a turning point for me. I began imagining our son blurring the separation between the world of ability and disability.

Tammy

The pain seemed to swallow me.

I had longed to know what was going on inside of my son in the days before his injury. That night, before Pat found me in Zach's room, I'd remembered that Zach often wrote random thoughts on sheets of paper that he stored between the pages of his Bible.

I'd pulled the book from his backpack, held Zach's Bible in both hands, and sat next to his bed where we had so often knelt to pray. Within the worn volume, I found a folded sheet of tattered paper with his familiar scrawl: "Ways to Glorify God."

Under Zach's subtitle "Servant Leading," he had written, "I want to start acting real and have a mind-set to be generous and give compliments. I would like to sit and hang out with whoever seems outcast."

In an age when it wouldn't be uncommon for a mom to find

evidence of bullying, drug use, depression, or risky relationships in a kid's backpack, I found evidence that reinforced what we had always known about Zach. He cared for people and wanted to make a difference in their lives. He detested phoniness and wanted to be more authentic. He saw a world in need and wanted to be more generous.

What does a person call a loss like this—not only a loss of who Zach had been to me, to our family, but to a whole community and beyond? Was it loss of *light*?

A section of paper stuck between the pages of Zach's Bible was titled "Journaling." His authenticity and genuine faith challenged me. He admitted his shortcomings and then continued, "God also brought to my attention that it is right to persevere for the sake of the One who persevered for me, [Christ]."

I read snatches of lyrics for a new song he was composing:

Such a beautiful satisfaction
I pray for the joy in your salvation.
Cause I've found new life, found new life.

Let me live to see you glorified.
Let me live to see you glorified.
Let my heart be opened wide.
Let me live to see you glorified.

If only I could have known the melody and chords of this unborn song so I could sing my son's words, sing his song with him. I would likely never know how he heard it in his mind while composing.

Sweet memories strengthened and crushed me simultaneously. I didn't want to leave his bedroom sanctuary, but in a way, I was too shaken to stay. That's how Pat had found me, crumpled and crying.

His willingness to enter into my misery with me that night helped in ways I couldn't express. Although it was pain we were sharing, we were in it together.

And *together*, Pat and I had read what Zach had penciled onto the walls of his room:

I count all things to be loss in view of the surpassing
value of knowing Christ Jesus my Lord, for whom I
have suffered the loss of all things, and count them
but rubbish so that I may gain Christ.

PHILIPPIANS 3:8, NASB

I am convinced that neither death, nor life, nor angels,
nor principalities, nor things present, nor things to
come, nor powers, nor height, nor depth, nor any other
created thing, will be able to separate us from the love
of God, which is in Christ Jesus our Lord.

ROMANS 8:38-39, NASB

My heart clenched over what Zach had accepted before it was demanded of him—*I have suffered the loss of all things*—and his pencil-scratch embrace of an unembraceable truth—*and count them but rubbish so that I may gain Christ.*

Pat and I wept together . . . and prayed. As he told me about the morning when Zach had wondered whether God would ever have him become like one of the children with disabilities we'd served in South Africa, we wept some more. Eventually, we made our way to bed and fell into an exhausted sleep.

My last conscious thoughts were of a prayer Zach had tucked into his Bible. According to its date, it had been written shortly before the accident:

Lord, I love you, and I need Your help to do so. I pray You would build in me a willing spirit to seek Your glory. I pray You would teach me how to glorify You.

The theme of the song he'd been writing.

Zach's spiritual maturity seemed to have outdistanced his age. God must have known he'd need to grow up fast in his faith.

Could my faith keep pace with his? Accepting? Embracing? Wanting God's glory more than I wanted to get back the Zach I knew?

Pat

With a portion of Zach's skullcap removed, his brain had unlimited room to expand.

As doctors began to wean Zach from the deep sedation and slowly wake him from his coma, I was struck by the extent and aftermath of what had happened inside Zach's brain. My crash course in brain science climaxed when a doctor breezed into Zach's room with the results of his recent CAT scan.

"Can you wait until my wife gets here? She's on her way. Took our youngest son, Soren, to school this morning. He's finding it hard to—. She'll be here any minute."

He couldn't wait. In an excruciatingly meticulous explanation, he told me what Zach's CAT scan revealed, noting in dispassionate detail each portion of my son's brain that had been injured and what those injuries would likely mean.

I so wished Tammy had been there to hear, or that the doctor had understood the need to wait until Tammy and I were together. How would I tell her? I couldn't imagine pulling off *dispassionate.*

The worst damage occurred on the left side of the brain, the surgeon said, suggesting that our aspiring Division 1 collegiate athlete would at the very least suffer significant weakness on the right side of his body. Our rugged, adventurous outdoorsman would also likely experience serious deficits of voluntary muscle motor control—like swallowing and controlling his bowels.

Significant damage to the occipital lobe indicated serious vision impairment. The list of *infarcts*—the medical term for brain tissue that died because of lack of blood flow—and their likely consequences continued ad nauseam. Literal nauseam.

What started as a prognosis began sounding more like an autopsy. I could hear my own ragged breaths.

Numbed and emotionally battered, concussed by what I'd heard, I listened to the young doctor's monotone. "And there appears to be an infarct in the Broca's area—the part of the brain that controls speech."

My heart muscle seemed to stop, forgetting what it was supposed to do.

Broca. An infarct in the Broca's area. He might not speak again. Not in front of large crowds, where he thrived. Not with his friends. Not in quick quips and jabs to his brothers or his sister. Not to Tammy or to me.

I might never again overhear Zach lovingly call Tammy "Peach." I might never again hear my oldest son call out, "Dad?"

The doctor had stopped talking and was looking at me for a response.

A response? His words had paralyzed me. "No, I . . . don't have any more questions right now."

With that, the doctor excused himself.

Tammy

After dropping off Soren at his school, I drove to the hospital to sit with Zach so Pat could pick up Chelsea at the airport. It had seemed only right to wait until Zach's condition stabilized before we flew her home to see her brother. Zach wouldn't have known if she'd come earlier and still might not. But now he was slowly waking from his coma, starting to respond in minute ways to stimuli. It was time.

When I walked into Zach's room, ready to hand Pat the keys, the look on his face frightened me.

"What's going on, Pat?"

"The doctor was here with the CAT scan results."

I'd missed hearing it in the doctor's own words. Couldn't it ever work out that I could be with a child who needed me without neglecting one of the others?

Chelsea's plane would be landing soon. So little time. Pat attempted to quickly explain what the surgeon had said.

Words. Too many words.

Sorrow brewed inside me.

Would I always be torn between my children's heartbreaks? Emotionally, Chelsea must have been devastated to have to navigate the early days of college while this drama unfolded so many miles away. I wanted to be the first one she saw at the airport—hugging her, feeling her body lean into mine, letting the silence between us communicate what neither of us could say.

But we'd decided that was Pat's role this time. And mine was to be with one of my other hurting children—the one with part of his skull missing, the one I may already have lost.

Pat

One task, then the next. One minute. Get through this minute.

Inching the car closer to the Arrivals sign at the airport, I focused on the assignment before me—how I would prepare my daughter to see her brother in his almost lifeless state. I felt as bruised as a boxer at the end of a pummeling match. A new depth of sadness, an aching sorrow, gripped me the moment I caught sight of Chelsea waiting at the curb outside the terminal.

Chelsea's brief smile showed how glad she was to be reunited with her family, even if only for a couple of days. But like a snuffed candle, the light vanished. She'd flown home for an incomprehensible reason—her brother's fight for his life. She fell into my embrace. Neither of us could talk. Maybe that was best.

The drive from the airport to the hospital was both too long and too short. We talked, but tiptoed around the questions that had no answers. She would start to chat about college life, then stop, as if conscious that her class load and the relationships she was making took a backseat to our current drama. I filled her in on the latest developments with Zach, intentionally softening some of the harsher edges.

I guided her through the hospital corridors that were too

familiar to me and foreign to her. When she saw Tammy, she hurried to her mother's arms.

When Chelsea finally stood at Zach's bedside, she attempted to smile at her brother, his glazed eyes now open and staring at hers. Her smile didn't last long. I ached for how my daughter was being hit full in the face with the reality we'd lived with daily since Zach's injury.

Again, sorrow rose within me—a force more and more difficult to contain. I held it in check throughout the morning visit, choking on emotion as Chelsea attempted to talk to a brother and best friend who continued to stare unresponsively.

When we left the hospital and drove to a nearby restaurant for lunch, I dropped Chelsea and Tammy at the entrance and left to find a parking space.

The moment their car doors closed, I began to weep uncontrollably. For the first time in my life I wailed and moaned with an emotional anguish unlike anything I'd experienced. It was as if seeing Chelsea's pain had given me permission to fully admit my own. I could no longer keep a cap on the well of grief roiling inside me. I surrendered to it.

My breakdown lasted only a few short moments. What happened next caught me completely by surprise. Letting the sorrow out had made room for consolation.

It trickled in. For the first time, I didn't resist.

CHAPTER

5

Pat

Almost a week since Zach's injury. Though Zach continued to emerge from the depths of the coma, he showed little response to our questions, and no real evidence of regaining normal function. He could lift his fingers from the bed or give a slow-motion thumbs-up. Little more.

Several friends had organized a prayer vigil for the Sunday afternoon of the weekend Chelsea spent at home. It was to be held in the gymnasium of our kids' school. I was both grateful for their kindness and grieved that there was a need for a prayer vigil at all. I had a hard time keeping it together in front of close friends, much less a large group.

Prior to the event, the organizers had asked if Tammy and

I would like to address the crowd coming in support of Zach. I'd turned to Tammy and said, "I'm too emotionally thin right now to be able to say anything."

"Don't you think we should?" Her face showed the battle between her desire to attend and exhaustion.

"If we feel led and strong enough to say something when the time comes, we can nod to the emcee. How does that sound?"

Tammy agreed.

The vigil, though somber, reminded us that we weren't alone and that Zach had influenced many lives. Music— including two of Zach's favorite songs—was followed by silent prayer and reflection. Several of Zach's school friends spoke about his far-reaching impact on their high school and the football team.

Mike, a leader on the football team, spoke with remarkable sensitivity to the audience, which was diverse in every way. He mentioned Zach's strong faith and said that in Zach he had met the one exception to the Christian idea of original sin—that since Adam and Eve, every human has been born with pre-existing sin, as St. Augustine proposed centuries ago. "Zach is simply the nicest and most selfless person I have ever known."

Mike pulled out his Bible and read what he had observed Zach reading a few months prior to his injury.

> Blessed are the poor in spirit,
>   for theirs is the kingdom of heaven.
> Blessed are those who mourn,
>   for they will be comforted.
> Blessed are the meek,
>   for they will inherit the earth.

Blessed are those who hunger and thirst
    for righteousness,
    for they will be filled.
Blessed are the merciful,
    for they will be shown mercy.
Blessed are the pure in heart,
    for they will see God.
Blessed are the peacemakers,
    for they will be called children of God.
Blessed are those who are persecuted because
    of righteousness,
    for theirs is the kingdom of heaven.

Blessed are you when people insult you, persecute you
and falsely say all kinds of evil against you because of
me. Rejoice and be glad, because great is your reward
in heaven.

MATTHEW 5:3-12

When Mike's tribute ended, the emcee glanced over to see
if Tammy and I wanted to add anything. I was readier than I
thought I'd be. The power of the school community that Zach
loved so much fed my courage to address these people who'd
been so faithful to hold our family in their hearts. Tammy and
I looked at each other, turned back toward the emcee, and
nodded in unison.

Tammy did exactly what I expect Zach would have done if
he had been there. She thanked everyone for coming and urged
them not to worry about Zach, but to work hard at school and
their sports.

I began by thanking Mike for his kind words about Zach. "But I want to assure everyone," I said, smiling, "that as Zach's parents, we're confident our son is definitely not exempt from original sin. And he would be the first to tell you that." The laughter that followed made it easier to breathe.

"I don't have to remind anyone here about Zach's free spirit, his fearlessness, and his prankster side. His antics are well known in this community. I don't have to elaborate with details about the day the police caught him on top of a house, using a slingshot to shoot paintballs at moving cars on the busy street below. Or about the time he set up a sound system on the roof so he and his makeshift band could entertain the neighborhood, whether they liked it or not."

More laughter.

"Or the day he tied a rope to the back of his grandfather's golf cart and had Nate pull him on his skateboard around the bustling streets of his grandparents' retirement community."

The crowd quieted again, but Mike's heartfelt Scripture reading rang in my ears. "I always found it strange," I said, "that Jesus would teach such an obvious paradox as the one Mike read to us: 'How happy are those who are sad.'

"I'm convinced Jesus did *not* mean that grief, sorrow, and loss are not real and not painful. In fact, I had a moment earlier this weekend in my car when overwhelming despondence washed over me."

I paused to collect myself. The audience paused with me.

"But what I experienced in the short time right after my eruption of sorrow and sobbing was deep and indescribable consolation. It came from realizing how my pain was pulling me into a story greater than my own—our own—the story of a

Father who had endured the suffering of His beloved Son and who felt, understood, and could sympathize with my pain."

An otherwise noisy gymnasium had never seemed so quiet.

"Zach prayed every day his freshmen year and many times since that God would use him to lead at least one classmate to God. I can assure you that God has used and is using Zach to lead me closer to the God he loves."

Tammy

Shortly before Chelsea's weekend visit, Zach had begun to come out of his medically induced coma, and I could finally look into his eyes.

Now, a few days later, we spoke without words. I again held my right cheek next to his as I had since he'd started to awaken. He was still intubated, so he could only sigh through closed lips. "Mmm—mmm—mmm." We were, in our own way, saying the same thing: "I love you."

He began to show that he could understand what we said and respond to some of the doctor's instructions. Progress. Not what we'd hoped. But we saw signs of life.

Almost two weeks later, after doctors removed Zach from the ventilator, I stood by the edge of his hospital bed with my guitar in hand. That past summer, in the dim light of the cement-block houses of the South African townships, Zach had taught me several new-to-me worship songs. Now my fingers formed the familiar chords as I sang his favorite, "From the Inside Out." I noticed Zach mouthing the words along with me. Then he shocked me by faintly singing: "Everlasting, Your light will shine when all else fades."

Hearing him form words—sing, however softly—thrilled me. Was it possible our son would recover far more than the doctors predicted? I continued to play guitar and tried to get Pat's attention. He was busy gathering our belongings.

"He's singing!" I said, as I kept playing, hoping with everything in me that Zach would not stop. Pat scrambled to find a camera to capture what we couldn't believe was happening.

My throat tightened. I could barely finish singing, the last words fading into a whisper. Pat and I wept, with gratitude this time. Zach was still here, and his soul was well.

∽

Hope is a great stabilizer, but that glorious moment of Zach's whispered singing didn't erase the crisis.

As the intensity of spending so much time in the ICU increased, I daily escaped to fresh air, sunlight, and the Charles River. I took Zach's iPod so I could listen to his favorite worship songs as I jogged past his red brick school, and then on the way back, past the monastery of the Society of Saint John the Evangelist.

The massive dappled sycamores that towered like sentinels along the river commanded my attention. Occasionally, I stopped to touch the jigsaw-puzzle bark. I saved fallen pieces to remember that day, that run, that break from the numbing times at the hospital. And to remind myself that we were seeing only a handful of pieces of the puzzle of Zach's recovery.

No one knew if this puzzle was made up of 250 pieces or a thousand. If Zach could form a word, would his entire vocabulary return? If he could squeeze my finger now, did that mean he'd soon be able to grip the neck of his guitar or dress himself? We couldn't look at the pile of puzzle pieces in front of us and imagine the finished picture.

He had improved, but not enough to start rehabilitation. He'd come back to us from the dismal abyss of his coma, but not far.

I couldn't imagine a more dramatic contrast between the young man lying on the hospital bed and the young man I'd scolded several years earlier after I'd asked him to quit playing with his brothers and clean his room.

"Zach, I'll be back in thirty minutes to check on your progress," I'd warned him one Saturday morning.

He'd promised he would get right on it.

I'd wondered if I should have been more specific about the definition of *clean*. But I left him to the task.

A half hour later, I nudged his door open and was greeted with the same mess, the same suspicious growing-boy sock odor, the same piles of clothes that weren't going to carry themselves to the washing machine.

"Zach, what did you promise me you'd take care of?"

"Mom," he'd said, covering his younger brother Soren's ears as the boy slept against Zach's chest. "Which is more important? Cleaning my room or comforting a crying baby?"

Bested by a kid with dirty socks and his priorities in order.

As I jogged along the familiar Charles River path, other memories crowded my mind: racing down mountain bike paths together, cheering as Zach executed 360s while kneeboarding, witnessing his fearless diving catches in football, sharing what we were learning about God, showing love to people of different nationalities and social standing, singing together with the children in South Africa, playing with orphans.

That's the Zach I wanted back. The son I knew and loved. But it seemed almost greedy to long for that. He was alive. Shouldn't I be grateful? How dare I say it wasn't enough?

We'd lost so much. Zach had lost so much, but no one could tell us how aware he was of all that had been taken from him. Lost, yet there he lay, in that hospital bed. There, but not fully there.

I ran, I cried, and I prayed. Day after day after endless day.

Sunlight often dazzled off the water. One day the surface of the water was glass; the next, ripples or waves, depending on the whim of the wind. Though the water's surface changed, the current below flowed unchanged.

On one run, I realized that, although the circumstances of our family had shifted drastically and the wind churned the surface into whitecaps at times, our beneath-the-surface *current*— our relationship with God—had remained and would remain constant.

Creativity and music had always been such connecting points between Zach and me. They disappeared with one look at my broken son the night of his injury. But now, as I ran, the beginnings of a new song were birthed in my mind.

BEAUTY IN SUFFERING

Hugs and loves and kisses good-bye, see you later tonight
Smiles and nicknames, a look in the eye, moments that
      bring such delight
Hello, then silence, a fast, quiet drive, a prayer, and
      peace is flowing

Lost and rushing we finally arrive, we say good-bye
  without knowing
Waiting, waiting, holding, holding

  Beauty in suffering calls out to me
  Beauty in suffering calls out to me
  Though everything changes, nothing really changes
  Though everything changes, nothing really changes
  You are there

Seasons pass, and some things are gone, but our love can't
  be broken
Held and carried, kept safe from the storm, by One who
  our love has spoken
We will wait and pray for you, our hearts are joined in
  a chorus
Holding fast to One who is true, holding to One who is for us
Praying, praying, hoping, hoping

  Beauty in suffering calls out to me
  Beauty in suffering calls out to me
  Though everything changes, nothing really changes
  Though everything changes, nothing really changes
  You are there

Running and crying and praying for him, music that
  pierces my soul
Sunlight that dances off waters I see, even the trees
  speak to me

Beauty in suffering calls out to me
Beauty in suffering calls out to me
Though everything changes, nothing really changes
Though everything changes, nothing really changes
You are there

∞

Pouring out lyrics on paper was somewhat cathartic, but it didn't satisfy my desire to reconnect with my son. For years, Zach and I had shared our thoughts during daily worship sessions together. As if he and I held a handle on opposite sides of an ancient water jar, we carried each other's hopes and dreams—what God wanted us to become and do in the world. We knelt side by side to pray for each other almost every night. The deep bond we shared as we worshiped God through prayer, singing, and playing our guitars—musically and spiritually in sync—was rare, I knew. That's what made its loss all the more devastating. Despite that brief moment singing with me after he emerged from the coma, a moment he hadn't repeated, it appeared Zach and I would never do those things again.

My mind struggled against the unthinkable.

Pat

Five weeks and six surgeries after an emergency helicopter carried our son's strong body from a football field to Boston's premier trauma center, nurses carefully wheeled a fragile fraction of that same body out the doors of the hospital. They then gently eased him into an ambulance that would transport him to Boston's Spaulding Rehabilitation Hospital.

Zach had lost nearly a third of his body mass—from 160 to 115 pounds. My son looked like an emaciated prisoner of war, with his shaved head, dark sunken eye sockets, and a never-changing dazed expression. He wore a protective helmet whenever he was out of bed, bore a portion of his skullcap in his abdomen—an awkward lump of bone—and had a feeding tube. Scars covered his torso where tubes had been inserted to drain infected fluid from his chest cavity during a four-week battle with pneumonia.

Even more unsettling—frightening—was the concave depression on the left side of Zach's head, surrounded by a large C-shaped incision held together with forty-five grotesque staples, industrial sized.

Zach arrived at Spaulding Rehab Hospital in rough shape. He couldn't walk, talk, or swallow food. He couldn't even sit up on his own. On his first day, three therapists were needed to maneuver his body into that position. He lacked the strength to keep his head straight when strapped upright. It fell limply from one side to the other. Drool poured out of both corners of his mouth. *My son. My son.*

Zach seemed to comprehend what people said to him and could even respond fairly quickly with subtle nods or by slightly shaking his head. But he rarely initiated any form of communication.

On the third night at the rehab hospital, we found a picture of a typewriter keyboard in the notebook that his speech therapist created for him. When it became clear that Zach was struggling to say something, we pulled out the keyboard and asked him to point to letters and spell the word he was trying to say.

Slowly he picked up his left hand and pointed to *D* and then *O*.

"Do?" I asked.

He did not nod but kept moving his hand, pointing to an *N* and then a *T*.

"Don't?" I tried again. This time Zach nodded subtly and slowly.

"Don't what, Zach? Keep going."

Could he communicate more than we'd imagined, but in a different way?

Zach painstakingly continued, pointing to a *G* and then an *O*.

"Don't go? We're not leaving, Zach. Don't worry," we assured him.

But he wasn't finished. He had more to say.

He looked down again and indicated more letters.

It quickly turned into a game of charades as we all tried to figure out what Zach was struggling to say.

Finally, we got it. Zach couldn't talk. But he had communicated his first full sentence. The perfect speech at the perfect time. A commencement address, if you will, that began his next journey—and ours—in earnest. His typed words revealed how much he remained the Zach we'd always known and loved.

The look on Tammy's face told me the sentence he wrote resonated through every fiber of her being too: "DON'T GO BACK TO AFRICA WITHOUT ME."

∞

South Africa seemed a long way off in those early weeks, yet I celebrated each small hint of progress as another reason to hope

Zach would someday return there, that he would defy all odds and experience a full recovery.

After his transfer to the Spaulding Rehab Center, we commuted into the heart of Boston every day for the next five months. Once in the bustling rehab hospital, we hopped onto a crowded elevator, presented our identification, and made our way to Zach's room. At least one of us spent all or part of every day with him, so our "circle" became the doctors, nurses, therapists, janitors, and friends who invested in helping him recover.

At some point in that long stretch, the routine became torturous for everyone else in our family. But somehow it energized me. I grew to love stepping through the doors of the hospital, and not—as my kids suggested—because of the irresistible aroma of the Dunkin' Donuts shop strategically located inside the hospital lobby. It was because I couldn't wait to be with Zach and see him conquer a small something he couldn't do the day before.

I watched one day as one of his therapists struggled to get Zach to grip the thick handle of a modified spoon. When Zach saw her flinch as she bent over him, his brow furrowed.

"It's okay, Zach," she said. "I twisted funny putting my son in his car seat this morning. It'll heal."

Zach wrestled his hand free from his assigned task, touched her on the shoulder, and tilted his head, his eyebrows tented in sympathy. Our son who couldn't yet hold a spoon had noticed someone's need and found a way to express comfort.

It was a win in my book.

If anything, Zach's physical gains lagged behind the subtle reemergence of his emotional and spiritual sensibilities and those qualities of character that demonstrated his love for others.

But he *was* making some improvement in his motor skills. To me, it felt like I was witnessing an ultra-slow-motion resurrection. Every incremental change fed the hope that Zach was on the way to a full recovery. The process became intoxicating for me.

Tammy saw things from a different point of view. I was the proud dad celebrating my seventeen-year-old son's newfound ability to swallow a teaspoon of water. Tammy was the heartbroken mother who focused on the bib that soaked up what dribbled out. I applauded when Zach grunted a response to my questions. Tammy mourned his regression from storytelling and songwriting to relying on almost infantile methods of communicating, as if nearly two decades of growth had been lost when he collapsed on the football field.

I found the rehab surroundings visible evidence of hope. Tammy saw the equipment and assists and straps and belts and therapies as evidence that something horrible had happened to our son.

And it had. She wasn't wrong.

Nate and Soren had grown hospital-weary too. I couldn't blame them. Tammy and I worked hard to make sure their physical needs were met. But emotionally, we barely had enough in us to stay afloat and manage the minute-by-minute responsibilities for a son who couldn't even hold his head up. At the time, I wondered why the rest of our family was becoming less interested in the one place that gave me any measure of comfort—Zach's room at the rehab facility.

I wasn't more devoted or dutiful than they were, than Tammy was. I drew strength from a place that sapped theirs. Was I supposed to tamp down my enthusiasm because they felt differently, because Tammy found the same setting drained her?

If I was the one-man cheering squad, Tammy was the prag-matist, the statistician, and the replay analyst. If I was Zach's rehab birthing coach, Tammy was the laboring mother who after months of pushing with excruciating contractions had made what seemed like no progress. If I was an unofficial mem-ber of his therapy team, Tammy was a detective, trying to make sense of the missing person who was her son, caught in the frus-tration of not knowing how to fill out the report. *Missing, but here. Not dead, but not what we expected living to look like.* Hope hovered, but what was it saying? Hold out for full recovery or find a way to navigate a nameless loss?

Tammy

It had no name. This aching loss. This chaotic vacuum—emptied of air itself but filled with noise and activity. The first weeks at the rehab hospital held a measure of exhilaration as we watched positive changes in Zach, small as they might have seemed to others. But there was no sudden healing.

Zach had to relearn everything—even eating, blended foods first, then soft ones. Finally, he could eat regular food, but it took him an hour and a half to finish even a simple meal. He'd graduated to sitting, then to standing for brief periods, then to walking with assistance. He had to be taught how to write again—first a word, then a phrase, then a sentence. The process was achingly slow.

How many staff members had it taken to help my son do what he'd first learned at six months old—sit up? How sad was it that we cheered over his relearning to swallow?

How much sadder if he hadn't?

Some parents in a similar situation might rail against God. He wasn't the object of my despairing thoughts. God was my tether to hope. I was confused by an invisible, unnamed *thing* that had virtually, if not actually, taken my son from me. It wasn't football, although my relationship with football at this point had grown dysfunctional.

Because of that sport, part of Zach's skull had been relocated. Part of me had gotten lost in the move—the part that had once been filled by a vibrant, exceptional, life-giving connection with my son's beautiful mind and expressive soul. I'd derived such joy from that closeness, from our conversations, from watching how his mind thought and how his faith was growing. All that had been silenced.

Loss commanded my attention. Loss, or trying to help Zach distance himself from it. This child of mine whose words and worship made the two of us kindred hearts now spoke in thick-tongued grunts.

Zach, I don't know what you said. I can't understand you.
I can't understand.

CHAPTER

6

Pat

Zach passed milestones every day, it seemed, on his long road toward recovery. Each one was the result of hundreds of hours of muscle retraining, brain rewiring, and expectation readjusting, for the staff and for us as a family. It wasn't unexpected that he became well-liked among the doctors, nurses, therapists, and especially the janitorial staff. His infectious, gaping smile—though lopsided—was a "skill" he used often.

And somehow, he still managed to make people laugh. He'd invented his own method of dealing with the drool he couldn't control. He stuck a washcloth in the corner of his mouth and let it hang there like some would dangle a toothpick. His rag answer looked ridiculous, laughable, but it worked. And it showed that something within him retained the ability to—at least on a minor level—recognize and solve a problem.

On her third visit home from college that fall, Chelsea apologized to Zach for coming straight from her field hockey game to the rehab center. No time to shower first. Zach slowly—everything he did was slow—reached for her hand and drew her close to his bedside. Chelsea thought he was bringing her in for another hug, but instead he raised her hand in the air, leaned toward her armpit, took a big whiff, and slowly verbalized as best he could, "Noooo . . . you . . . smell . . . greaaaaat." That was our Zach. Humor and love intact.

Weeks passed. When Tammy and I stepped away from the hospital for work or Nate's and Soren's school activities, the care team occasionally strapped Zach into a wheelchair so he could move around the hallway on his own, using his feet to pull himself along. He loved patrolling the floor, waving at other patients and occasionally scooting into a room to give a patient his awkward version of a high five. He earned the title "Mayor of the 5th Floor." His meandering became so routine that one patient reportedly could not go to sleep without saying good night to Zach.

But no one could tell us how far back Zach would come. If he'd made this much progress, could we expect him to double that in a few more months? Would something click someday and restore him whole, a slower but strong version of himself?

I pacified myself with possibilities as I sought answers to those questions. Maybe others saw me as naively optimistic, or maybe it was our family's long history of sports training. But I was energized watching my son scoot down the hallway while strapped into a wheelchair, convinced more progress would come, given enough time and intense training. Athletes overcome odds. I was living in the middle of what could be the ultimate underdog comeback story.

On Tammy's face, I saw heartbreak over the same scene.

We weren't on the same page. I attributed it to the aftermath of the traumatic event that had caused all the upheaval. Our relationship had always thrived on the interplay of different personalities, the depth it brought to any conversation. Now, though, I felt another response brewing.

Love hadn't disappeared. Intimacy survived somehow. But our opposite approaches to what consumed us felt like an intruder in our marriage. I longed for Tammy to be as happy as I was with Zach's progress. She'd feel better about everything if she joined my "Our son is holding his head up all by himself!" victory lap.

Tammy

Sadness greeted me at the entrance to the rehab hospital every single time I walked through its doors. Zach was there, alive but not himself, because we had let him—encouraged him—to play football.

Pat saw the sport differently.

We've always respected each other's personality differences and individual gifts. But it began to grate on me that after all Zach had been through, after how radically our lives had been altered, Pat remained infatuated with football.

I'd heard it often enough that I could parrot his speech almost word for word. Football builds character: dedication, discipline, determination, perseverance, strength, toughness, and a healthy work ethic, he often said. What other sport brings together such a wide variety of body types and skills, and then melds a bunch of individuals into a team? In a country like ours, which is so radically individualistic, you can't find a sport that gives people (both players and fans) the experience of camaraderie and community the way football does.

Really, Pat? And you can still say that when you're feeding Zach ice chips on a spoon because he can't do it himself? What future did football make possible for our son?

I knew about kids and accidents—on the playground, bike riding, goofing off in the backyard, and in sports. I knew kids could break arms and legs, but I didn't know they could break brains.

And we'd signed Zach up for this. We'd paid for his cleats. Cheered him from the sidelines. Celebrated aggressive play.

As parents and fans, we'd assumed every precaution was being taken to minimize injury potential. That's what football helmets were for. I heard my own voice resonating from past games. *Nice hit!* The replay wouldn't leave me alone.

Had I read it or seen it on video recently, or had it been one of Zach's surgeons who told us that a helmet can only protect the skull, and imperfectly at that? The brain is like the egg yolk inside of an eggshell. If it gets battered, shaken hard enough, nothing can keep it from scrambling.

In any hard hit, no human invention can protect the brain.

And no human invention can protect a family from the fallout.

Pat

As curious as it might sound, after nine-plus years in the city, no single factor contributed more to making me feel at home in Boston than the people who gathered around us in our time of crisis—beginning with Zach's football coach.

Before making his daily appearance in the doorway of Zach's room, Coach Papas's deep, gravelly, ground-shaking voice—as he greeted nurses and patients along the way—awakened Zach from his between-therapy-session naps. At the sound of Coach's voice, Zach's eyes brightened, his body stiffened to attention, and he looked toward the door with eager anticipation—ready to report for his daily workout.

As the weeks crawled by, Zach's football team also passed significant milestones, without our son's presence. Football had not been a prominent sport at Zach's school. Though the inimitable Coach Papas had injected new life into the program, Zach's high school had not won a championship in fifty years. Most years, in fact, they'd had more losses than wins.

After Zach's incident, the team decided to dedicate their season to their fallen player—and that collective decision seemed to inspire and energize the players and coaches. Wins began to pile up, along with expectations and the resolve to win a championship to honor Zach.

But even if they could manage to stay undefeated for the remaining games of the season, the final contest would pit them against the number one team in New England's Independent School League.

This opponent consistently won games by more than thirty points. The number one team's program became so dominant that one of their opponents forfeited a game against them out of fear that the overwhelming size, speed, and talent of this prep-school football powerhouse could seriously injure their players.

That reminder seemed to hit Tammy especially hard. I saw it

as evidence that the sports world made every effort to minimize risks for young players. Tammy saw it as evidence that football had become too great a risk.

She cited Zach as proof.

With such a dominating opponent several games away from squaring off with Zach's team in the last game of the year, the dramatic end toward which this season seemed to be moving looked less like a David-and-Goliath battle and more like an opportunity for a moral victory. Like Rocky Balboa in the first *Rocky* movie, success came not from winning but from showing up and not getting knocked out.

Coach Papas suggested an even more compelling possibility for a storybook ending to a dramatic season—getting Zach well enough to join his teammates on the sidelines for the final game. Tammy and I couldn't think of anything more encouraging—for all of us—than to have Zach present at a game with that much at stake, reunited at least in spirit with his teammates.

As Zach's high school's fairy-tale football season drew to a close, their projected showdown with the number one team became reality. Zach had continued making steady gains in his recovery. But despite the coach's idealistic vision of Zach cheering from the sidelines, our son was still months away from being discharged from the rehab hospital.

Doctors and therapists had trained us to transport Zach from bed to wheelchair and from wheelchair to car and back again. That allowed us to take him off the floor and outside for fresh air every day. We were even permitted to take Zach on short drives.

He may not have been ready to check out of rehab for good,

but when the night of the game finally came, we believed Zach was ready to leave for two hours to watch that crucial game.

Despite our constant badgering and his primary doctor's agreement that both we and Zach could handle it, we were never able to get formal permission to take Zach to the game before she left the country on vacation. Neither did we get a firm denial of permission. But on game night, the on-call doctor told us, "I'm sorry, but I do not feel comfortable with this." We were devastated.

She knew we could safely transport Zach. We assured the doctor of the extreme measures we had taken to ensure Zach's safety. We let her know about the indoor press box secured to keep him warm and prevent him from being overwhelmed by scores of classmates and parents who would swarm him if he showed up at the game. We responded to every objection she made, but she refused to sign off.

Our haggling continued for over an hour. The game had already started, and we were stuck at the hospital. But when the on-call doctor finally left, we determined we would too— with Zach.

None of the staff found it unusual that I pushed Zach out of his room in his wheelchair. Or even that I took him down the elevator. Heading out for their evening "walk," they might have assumed. If anyone questioned where we were going, they kept it to themselves.

I rolled my son out the exit to where Tammy waited in the getaway vehicle, and we bolted for the football field.

We arrived at the field with a minute left in the first half, and the game tied 7 to 7. We weren't going to make it inside and upstairs to the relative safety of the press box—away from the clamor of the fans and Zach's friends—before halftime. The community member who'd helped arrange our clandestine operation motioned us through a back door right behind the concession stand. He assured us we could get through the corridor to the stairs that led to the press box from this back entrance.

Within seconds we could hear the clacking of football cleats slapping down the concrete corridor. We hadn't known the hallway in which we stood intersected with the entrance to the locker room.

When the first home team player reached the door and began pulling it open, he noticed us in the shadows ten yards down the hall. He locked eyes with Zach and froze. His face lit up, and so did Zach's.

With a train of teammates impatiently piling up behind him, the player let out a gasp. The sudden pause caught the attention of the young man behind him, who also looked our direction. One by one, each player, manager, and coach glanced our way, astonished. Some mouthed or said, "Zach!" as they stepped into the locker room.

Coach Papas was the last to reach the intersection. The "we're tied and that's not going to cut it" ticking time bomb that was about to explode on his players inside the locker room fizzled once he saw the wide-eyed smile and frantic, awkward wave of the player to whom the team had dedicated the season.

The need for Coach Papas to work his players into a frenzy and say something that would inspire them to play the best half of football of their lives vanished when Zach appeared—unintentionally—a few feet from the entrance to the locker room. Zach's presence spoke louder than even Coach Papas could yell, and he knew it.

He simply told his players, "No one wants to be out on that field more than Zach does. He can't play for himself tonight, but you can play for him."

∞

At 8:45 that night, a giant lay slain on a high school gridiron near Boston. For the first time in fifty years, Zach's high school completed an undefeated football season and won the Independent School League championship.

At 9:15, the soft *ding* of the elevator echoed off the walls of the quiet fifth-floor corridor of Spaulding Rehab Hospital. When the elevator doors opened, we stealthily wheeled Zach past the nurses' station, down the long hallway, and back into his room, where we quickly lifted him into his bed. As he lay back on a pillow and closed his eyes, his arms refused to let go of the only evidence that he had gone on more than a wheelchair ride around the hospital that night.

He fell asleep smiling and cradling the game ball.

Tammy

Despite my newly complicated relationship with football, I think I needed that victory more than the team did.

Nothing normal had marked our trip to the football field. Zach wasn't suited up. He was in a wheelchair he couldn't get into on his own. But he'd connected with his teammates. They hadn't forgotten him. Zach was still inspiring others, despite his limitations.

We weren't in control of anything those days. But for a

couple of hours, we had our son back and witnessed an odds-defying, decades-of-defeat-busting victory over an impossible opponent. The hope encased in that win—and in the winning game ball Zach clutched—wasn't lost on me.

7

Tammy

"Why do you keep dragging me to hospitals? I am so sick of hospitals."

Eleven-year-old Soren spilled out his lament as I tucked him into bed one night during the third month of Zach's recovery.

Soren was angry with us—and he had a right to be. Three days before Zach was injured, we'd made him change schools. Soren had to process all the pain of the fallout from the incident in a place where he knew no one, his own version of what Chelsea had to go through a thousand miles from us. Zach had been the older buddy Soren turned to with his angst. But Zach wasn't available. And neither were we.

"Soren, I don't like hospitals either. But this is Zach's best hope to get better. I know it's hard on you. I'm sorry, Sor—"

"And why did you put me in a new school? That's not fair."

"I'm sorry for that, too. We wanted the best school for you, but now you're dealing with hard stuff in a place with no friends."

He turned his face to the wall and curled up as he had when a toddler. "I wish this hadn't happened to him. To any of us."

Upheaval swirled around our family from every direction. Nate's and Chelsea's worlds had been stripped of normalcy too.

It took Soren's well-deserved rant, his honesty, to help me more fully acknowledge my own exhaustion and how it had impacted all of us. The rehab hospital visits weren't getting easier for me or the kids.

Pat and I had returned to a regular work schedule during the day. Every night—*every night*—we took Soren and Nate with us to the hospital to eat dinner with Zach. It started with an hour and a half of watching Zach feed himself with all the finesse of a toddler. As grateful as we were for the progress, the gap between who he'd been and who he was now remained wide and obvious.

And I had to relearn how to parent—both my injured son and my injury-affected other children. Each of them would retreat into silence and then voice their displeasure with the unfairness of it all—how much time Zach was consuming, how often Pat and I couldn't be there for them the way we wanted to, and the ways their lives had been thrust into an upheaval they hadn't signed up for.

Chelsea and Zach had been so close. What could they share now? Soren had leaned on Zach, but now Soren, six years his junior, was the stronger of the two. Nate had lost not only one of his closest friends, but his most respected role model at the vulnerable age of fourteen.

Family night took on a whole new meaning during those weeks in the rehab hospital. Our evenings together weren't completely devoid of fun. The boys found Zach's drool solution hilarious. They still found ways to tease each other.

Zach and his brothers connected through video games on the big-screen TV in the family lounge. We'd never been fans of video games, but the brain surgeon said playing might help improve Zach's eye-hand coordination, balance, and mental agility. Nate and Soren competing with each other and with Zach—the three laughing together—restored a temporary link among the boys that had been shelved since Zach's injury.

"I love this," Pat said as the boys jostled for what they considered the superior game controller.

"Hand it over, Zach," Nate said. "It's my turn."

Zach turned his head side to side in a subtle figure eight. "Nooo . . . myyy . . . tuuuuurn."

His grip strength usually won the battle, unless his brothers succeeded in ambushing him from behind. Nate and Soren were considerate of Zach's needs but unwilling to let him play his sympathy card, not that Zach would have tried. In the moment, they were just brothers.

I loved it too.

We told stories, played Connect Four, took turns pushing Zach in his wheelchair, and snuggled with Zach in what I referred to as his "African tent bed," so named to convince Zach to sleep in its confines. He narrowed his eyes when his brothers tried a little too hard to tout the tent's "cool" features.

The large crimson rectangle with walls of black net and humongous zippers could only be opened from the outside, for his protection. Making decisions and processing consequences are brain functions that are slow to return in cases like Zach's, if they ever do. His impulse control was a problem as well. The African tent bed was designed to keep our brain-injured "escape artist" from wandering and injuring himself when unattended.

Zach had never been a fan of restrictive devices. Because of earlier attempts to get out of bed on his own, which would have been a huge danger for him, at bedtime he now had his arms in braces, his hands encased in boxing-glove style mittens to keep him from scratching his surgical wounds, guardrails on both sides, and the tent over his bed.

As we stepped outside his room after tucking him in, we often heard him ripping off the Velcroed boxing-glove mitts. How someone with so little physical agility could manage that act baffled the hospital staff.

Pat said it didn't surprise him. It didn't surprise either of us. We knew Zach.

On the rare nights when Nate and Soren didn't come to the hospital, I sang worship songs with Zach and sometimes danced with him to his favorite worship songs. He was so frail physically—vulnerable to falling or injuring himself because of his unsteadiness. So we slow danced, with careful movements as I held him upright. Somehow, the connection with him held *me* upright. I felt a closeness with both Zach and God as we danced and worshiped.

I enjoyed those alone times with him at the end of the day, and judging by his facial expressions, Zach did too. But as it does for any parent working all day and spending every night at their child's, spouse's, or parent's hospital bedside, the complicated and endless routine also drained me.

Pat and I began alternating nights at the hospital—one parent staying home with Nate and Soren and one going to see Zach. No one liked fragmenting the family, but survival dictated our actions. And it reminded Soren and Nate that their interests and needs mattered to us.

We also set up a schedule for friends to visit Zach on the weekends so we could manage a few hours of respite. I coordinated the routines to keep us functioning, but organizing this schedule depleted my energy even more.

The "I am so sick of hospitals" talk with Soren brought home how difficult it was to grieve the loss of one child while mothering three others, and how hard it was to parent our other children the way I wanted while grieving. There is no "win" in that sentence or sentiment. Zach's needs seemed overwhelming. I didn't want the other three to think I considered their concerns trivial. Or that Zach was more important. It was the *chronic versus acute* problem, the triage dilemma—*Who's bleeding out at the moment?* Sometimes the answer was me.

I saw that familiar exhaustion in the eyes of other families caring for someone at the rehab hospital. The mother of a car accident victim left just shy of brain-dead. The woman whose husband's stroke left him in a condition similar to Zach's in many ways, but in the body of a man with whom she'd shared life for fifty years. I couldn't imagine the heartache their families were experiencing. Even though I empathized with them, I didn't dare take on their grief too.

Like Zach, Nate would sometimes gather me in his arms for a dance—a brief but welcomed distraction from the sadness I felt inside. I craved that intimate connection with all my kids. But I was so weighted with sorrow that I could barely move across the floor.

And I sensed a growing distance between Pat and me. Though we'd been comfortable with our differences before, we saw the situation with Zach from opposing perspectives. I couldn't understand Pat's uncontainable optimism. And I was convinced he couldn't begin to understand the depth of my sorrow.

Sadness over this all-consuming, indefinable sense of loss tore a larger and larger hole in my soul.

It followed me even on those rare occasions when we were able to spend time with Nate and Soren away from the hospital. I wanted to enjoy time with the two of them on a ski lift one day, but my attention was drawn below us as I watched teen boys perform tricks Zach used to do with ease. Every family moment we had together was a reminder that Zach wasn't there.

One night, after running along the river, I came home crying.

"Are you okay, Mom?" Nate and Soren asked in unison.

I sank to the floor. They joined me. My sons' arms around me—I can't begin to describe the comfort.

"It's going to be all right, Mom," Soren said, patting my back.

I caught the look Nate sent Soren before saying, "We'll get through this."

No more words were necessary.

As my sons held me, offering me the comfort I too often hadn't been able to offer them, I was reminded of one of my favorite images of the Christ child and His mother, the child reaching a dimpled hand to quiet His mother's tears. The child comforting His mother.

But Chelsea. My Chelsea. She missed out on the community support we received, the daily though strained family interactions. Her words from a few weeks earlier penetrated my soul: "You think it's hard to lose a son? I lost a brother *and* a best friend."

Even when I flew to Tennessee to watch her field hockey games, my mind was distracted by music echoing from the adjacent football field as the team warmed up.

Our children lost not only a brother, but for too long a mother and father as well. We spent as much time with them as we could, but the multileveled weariness wore away at us in those months as we focused on Zach's recovery.

I longed for Nate and Soren to tell me how they were doing, but they didn't talk much about *their* loss.

"Nate, come on. I'm listening," I'd insist.

But more frequently, he found reasons to be on the phone or go out with a friend even when I was around.

"Soren, can we talk? How are you doing?"

"Fine. I've got to finish my homework now."

And so it went.

It became all the more obvious that people—no matter their age or what brought them to that place—grieve in different ways and on different timetables. I learned to accept my kids' silence and tried to listen when they did want to talk.

While life wavered on the home front, the rehab hospital staff set up a meeting to talk about next steps for Zach. I will never forget that meeting. Each staff member around the table reported Zach's gains but made one thing clear.

He was not going to be able to move home.

Hearing that Zach would most likely never work or live alone was difficult for both Pat and me. What devastated us even more was their prognosis that Zach's ability to speak would be severely impaired . . . for life.

I didn't hear anything the therapists said after that. Though it was obvious Zach's speech was still garbled, very slow, and hard to understand, I'd believed it would improve. This dose of crippling reality was a crushing blow. I couldn't imagine not being able to really talk with him or hear him freely share his heart and passion or listen to his clear voice lifted in worship.

If I thought I'd known the dregs of sadness before, I soon found the pit was deeper than that.

Pat

He wouldn't be coming home?

The rehab team might as well have been wearing boxing gloves for the bruising I took with that statement. Zach couldn't live at home? It had been the goal toward which we'd been working so hard since his injury. I wanted him home, where he belonged, despite the challenges that would bring.

"We can put in special safety features," I said. I'm sure I interrupted someone's statement about yet another life goal Zach would never reach. But I couldn't imagine not having Zach home. Unacceptable.

One of the therapists said, "You have to understand how much care your son will need."

"We'll hire someone," I said, looking to Tammy. Her face registered the shock coursing through my body. "We can hire professional help to . . . live at the house and continue his therapy there. We can—" I ran out of words.

"Pat, Tammy, your son's best chance of a strong recovery is for him to move to a residential brain injury school. His needs are too great to be handled at home."

My optimism took a nosedive. Tammy stared at the team as if she were having as hard a time as I was comprehending what we'd been told.

No amount of persuasion would change the inevitable.

Over the next two months we spent scores of hours researching and visiting many schools and residences and lining up funding for Zach's care. The financial burden was a reality, but we refused to focus on that concern. Whatever it took, whatever Zach needed, we'd have to find a way.

I could see the hurt in Tammy's eyes when we talked about the college scholarships we should have been applying for instead of frantically searching for financial aid to keep our son in diapers.

At length, we concluded that the May Center School for Brain Injury and Neurobehavioral Disorders was the best school for Zach. But it was also the farthest away. Another major transition was on the horizon. His football injury had in so many ways distanced him from us, and our family members from one another. Now his caregiving needs were about to increase that distance.

CHAPTER

8

Pat

I knew a long and difficult journey lay before Zach. Like Tammy, I grieved that the next leg of that venture would occur at the May Center School nearly an hour south of our home, rather than *in* our home. Our family's daily trek to Spaulding Rehab Hospital was ending. I would no longer see Zach every day. Being near him had kept me stable, tethered to something real. Involved in his healing. Engaged in the process. Working the plan.

But the plan had disintegrated. Now I'd see him only on weekends. Someone else would watch for the daily nuances of change it had been my joy to catalog. I couldn't shake the feeling we'd be dropping him off at an orphanage and would need permission to visit on the weekends.

Somehow Tammy and I and the other kids had made it through a good chunk of the school year, kept up with most of our responsibilities, and practiced the art of focusing on the task at hand, whatever that was.

Despite everything clamoring for our attention, despite our conversations about Zach so often happening on different wavelengths, Tammy and I had tenaciously maintained our two-decades-long commitment to weekly date nights—dinner out, a walk or bike ride along the Charles River, a show at the theater. It took everything in us to hold on to that commitment when so much was falling apart and time was at a premium.

We'd carefully designated disagreements off-limits on date night. A relationship-saving move. We hadn't stopped loving each other, hadn't stopped caring about what mattered to the other person. But we also couldn't deny that the air hung heavy between us. Some might wonder how we could pull that off— sitting face to face or walking side by side when our thoughts took such different paths regarding Zach and his future.

All I can say is that we took the idea of commitment to each other seriously. We'd been counseled early in our marriage to hold on to the weekly date night concept no matter what, even if it required—as it did during this season of life—turning date nights into date breakfasts or lunches so as to avoid additional time away from the other kids when they were home from school.

Lately, the dates hadn't been fun, but they did keep us connected despite our disconnect.

"The Indian buffet, Tammy?"

"Sounds good."

"Want to walk? We might not get another warm day like

this for a while." I knew before she answered that this would be the only situation in which my fast-moving wife would choose slow over fast.

"Let's walk."

"You should get a warmer coat," I suggested.

"I'm fine. It's gorgeous outside."

"I'll grab another coat for you."

"I don't need it," she called as I ran up the stairs.

"I'm getting it for myself."

The sounds of the city reverberated around us during the short walk that would take us to one of our favorite restaurants on the second floor of a restored storefront in Harvard Square.

"How was your meeting with your guys this morning, Pat?"

"Great. We have some incredible student leaders. I wish I had more time to give to them. How was your staff meeting at the church?"

With a heavy sigh, Tammy responded, "Well, J.D.'s leaving."

"What? You're kidding me."

"He was offered a senior pastor position in Denver."

"I guess I'm happy for him, but the boys loved him as their youth pastor. One more loss for Nate and Soren."

Tammy slowed her steps. "I guess we don't have to rush, do we."

I matched her pace. "Not today."

"That's . . . good. Rushing isn't healthy for any of us."

"Sounds like curious counsel," I said, "coming from a runner."

She slipped her hand into mine. "I don't run for speed."

"I know."

"I'm cold," she said, moving even closer.

I swung the backpack off my shoulder and pulled out her fleece jacket, "Here."

"I thought you said you were getting a coat for yourself."

"In case you haven't noticed, it's mid-February in Boston and the sun is going to set in about two hours. It may be sunny, but it's not warm."

"Thanks," she said and moved in even closer.

Those dates together often closed some of the intangible distance between us, if only for a few hours. Then it was back to our packed routines, the call of our work schedules, caring for our children, and the needs of the child who wasn't coming home.

The fulcrum was off-center again. Zach wouldn't need us every day.

But I needed him.

On the morning of the move on February 23, my frail, six-foot, 145-pound traumatic brain injury survivor limped out the door of the rehab hospital. His skullcap was freshly reattached where it belonged. His hair had grown long enough to cover most of his scar. He'd regained thirty pounds. I'd tracked every one of them during his daily weigh-in that followed our nightly dinner and shower routine, and our doughnut indulgence. Our rhythm of life was about to be reset again. I still held out hope that much more recovery lay ahead.

Tammy

At Spaulding Rehab, I'd asked Zach, "How do you feel now about what happened to you?"

He'd typed an answer on his keyboard: "I am not very

pumped, but I am ABSOLUTELY SURE THAT THE LORD HAS A PURPOSE FOR IT!!!"

What faith. I clung to his confidence as, with his belongings piled floor to ceiling in two cars, we slowly and solemnly made our way down the freeway to Zach's new residential rehab school—the May Center School for Brain Injury and Neurobehavioral Disorders. Pat led in the first car. As I drove the second car, Zach and I listened to songs we had played and sung together in South Africa.

Hearing the music, I could envision four South African orphans squealing with delight as they hung on to Zach, two on each arm. Three weeks before the injury, he told me he wanted to move to South Africa after college and work with AIDS orphans in townships. Now instead of prepping him for college and a career ministering to orphans, we were moving him to a group home for the brain injured.

I focused on the road ahead, but my thoughts jetted back to a few days earlier, when I'd asked how he felt about his new brain injury school. It took a while for him to force out the words, but he said he really wanted to go back to his old high school instead. I explained that he wouldn't be able to take in new information at that school until his short-term memory returned. He was happy to hear that the goal of his new "brain" school was to prepare him to return to his school as soon as possible.

I held such a tentative grip on that hope that it scooted out of reach as I followed Pat's car toward the May Center group home. Suddenly I was crying so hard, I almost had to pull to the side of the road. The rest of the drive blurred past. Zach alternated between staring out the window and laying his head on my shoulder.

When we arrived at Zach's new home, the staff members and four residents greeted us. They interacted with Zach in the living room while we connected with the manager in the kitchen.

When any of our kids headed to school for the first time, I was excited for what they'd learn, how they'd grow, the stories they'd have to tell. But here, in this live-in facility for those whose brains *weren't* on the precipice of lifelong learning and an upward trajectory of knowledge and skill development, my soul was rattled. It felt more like . . . being forced to surrender our son for adoption. Our seventeen-year-old, broken, stitched, stapled son.

The manager said all the right things, I'm sure. I hoped Pat would remember the details of what was discussed during that introduction. Handing over my son to someone else's care for who knew how long disconnected me from the moment. My mind drifted like early morning haze meandering across a familiar stretch of the Rocky Mountains. Although my body sat in the room, the rest of me was on a Montana trail, trying to keep four kids under ten from running too far ahead of me.

Pat and I often bookended our four on outdoor activities when they were that young. One of us took the lead, and the other remained at the back of our tribe. We hoped this was adequate protection from all the trouble they could individually or corporately get into as we hiked or biked, taking advantage of one of the myriad ways a kid could burn off energy.

Reality interrupted my daydream. I caught a word or two of what the manager was saying, but it was as if I were listening to her through a cement wall or a bad cell phone connection. Pat was leaning forward, nodding, paying attention. Good.

Because I couldn't. I wasn't processing the present. The past had me in its grip.

Zach as a precocious homeschooled kindergartner. A young, reckless teen clinging to the back of a truck. Suited up in his football uniform. Lying on a gurney, his cleated feet hanging over the end.

That scene jolted me back to the present. Our current situation. Zach wouldn't improve enough to live with us. We were inadequate for his care and recovery. He needed professionals. I'd lost another battle—the goal of bringing him home.

After the preliminaries, Pat and I walked into Zach's bedroom at the group home. Everything about it screamed *unfamiliar*. A decent room, but nothing resembling his space in the apartment at our house where we'd envisioned him spending the rest of his recovery time.

I couldn't process that we were going to have to leave Zach here, almost an hour from home. We hauled load after load into his new room and began to put clothes in his closet and dresser while he watched, unable to enter into the process. My actions were involuntary. *Put this here. Put that there.* Nurturing and nesting were far from my mind. *We have to leave him here.*

Because of Zach's short-term memory issues, we had to frequently remind him that this was his new house where he needed to stay to have the strongest possible recovery. He was happy to hear that he would come home to live with us on weekends. A few minutes later, we'd have to explain it all again.

We filled Zach's room with familiar items—banners, posters, pictures, and gifts his friends had brought to the hospital. We added photos of our family on the wall by his bed. On his dresser, we propped a photo album of South Africa images, a book of notes from his school friends, his Bible, and his iPod. As I set each item down, I waited for a surge of hope within me. It never came.

We'd assumed moving Zach would take all afternoon and evening, and it did. We hadn't anticipated how long it would take to say good-bye. Pat and I hugged and kissed him in his bedroom, then again in the residents' common living room, and again at his front door. We kept waving as Zach stood in the front doorway of "his" house while we drove away.

Two separate cars. Two different directions.

Pat felt it was important to stay with Zach at his new home that first night to make sure everything went smoothly. The school's policy wouldn't permit that. But a dear friend from church who lived nearby offered to let Pat stay at his place. It was a compromise Pat could live with. So he headed in the direction of our friend's house.

And I drove home in tears. Alone.

Again.

∞

The school suggested we have Zach stay at the May Center group home seven days a week for the first two weeks until he'd adapted to his new surroundings. When we were finally able to have him home with us on weekends, it quickly became evident that we would need to make changes and adaptations.

One of the looming changes felt so emotionally daunting that I postponed it until it couldn't be ignored.

Months after Zach's move to the May Center, I knelt on Zach's closet floor in our home and reluctantly handed a dozen slippery basketball jerseys to my mom, who knelt beside me. She and Dad had driven eight hours from Pennsylvania to help us make the next steps of the transition, physically and emotionally, from the rehab hospital to Zach's residential school.

We needed to clean out Zach's closet of the remnants of his previous activities and replace them with new items he now needed. Everything that had filled his closet for so long was now unnecessary and a painful reminder.

As Mom patiently folded and stacked the blue and white basketball jerseys, I was consumed with visions of Zach's graceful but passionate style of play. What once was and would never be again. Everything—every item we touched—became an emotional trigger.

The varsity lacrosse jerseys came out next. The start of the spring season was less than a month away. Zach wouldn't be part of it.

I reached for the football jerseys last. My stomach turned as I passed them to my mom. Coach Papas had once believed Zach had a chance to play in the Ivy League. Every dream—every single one—was gone.

My hands froze midmotion. "I can't do this anymore."

The look in my mom's eyes told me this was just as difficult for her as it was for me. "Are you sure you want to get rid of all these?" she asked.

She knew me. She could read what was going on inside of me—trying to let go and hold on at the same time. Of all people, Zach's grandmother—my mom—could empathize with the incomprehensible dichotomy. Zach was alive. But he wasn't the same. And never would be. What was wrong with me that my grief had no defined edges? *He's here. He's not here the same way. And he's not here in our home.*

"Let's set a few aside to keep but get rid of the rest," I said.

The deeper we dove into the task, the deeper our hearts sank into the reality that no aspect of life was untouched by what had happened to him, to us. Life moved forward. Work, meals, laundry, meetings, school events, friends, social gatherings, church . . .

And so we filled another trash bag with items Zach would never use again.

Football pants, pads, gloves, and shoes. The game-day white cleats we had purchased for Zach earlier that school year were still spotless. I handed them to my mom with funeral-like solemnity. Maybe we could donate them to our son's former high school for students who couldn't afford to buy their own.

When I picked up the receiver gloves Zach wore the night of his injury, I stopped to smell them. They seemed sacred. The life he'd known, the one I'd counted on and reveled in, had been taken from him that fateful night. I needed something tangible of Zach-before-his-injury, so I kept the gloves he'd worn when—under his own power—he'd stepped onto that scrimmage field.

"Something is *over*," Nicholas Wolterstorff writes in *Lament for a Son*. "Especially in places where he and I were together this sense of something *being over* washes over me." He suggests that what might be over is "happiness as the fundamental tone of my existence. Now sorrow is that. Sorrow is no longer the islands but the sea."

Wolterstorff's thoughts resonated with me. No longer the islands but the sea itself.

Once emptied of athletic gear, the closet mocked the empty ache I felt for the Zach I once knew. But the most traumatic part of the closet redo was yet to come.

I took several deep breaths and attempted to reason with the brokenhearted mother within me. This task, as with the many others we had undertaken in the last months, couldn't be avoided.

When I regained my focus, I reluctantly said, "Okay, hand them to me."

My mom teared up but said nothing. She passed me a stack of adult diapers.

"This is crazy," I said, as the textured exterior of the diapers rubbed against my hands. Mom handed me stack after stack, each one a reminder that this basic need was beyond Zach's ability to control, and that it might remain that way for the rest of his days.

It was a cruel reminder that our son was no longer a boy coming into his prime. So many dreams he'd had, so many dreams we'd entertained with him, lay in bulging black garbage bags.

CHAPTER

9

Pat

Five o'clock each Friday, Zach's brain school van pulled up to our house. It was my favorite moment of the week. I lived to watch Zach's face light up when he saw me; hear his high-pitched, siren-like squeal; feel his arms around me, squeezing me with strength no one knew he had as he lunged out of the car. I found it intoxicating. Addicting.

But the challenges of keeping Zach safe from five o'clock on Friday to eight o'clock Sunday night when I pulled up to the door of the May Center residence made Sunday night the *second* most welcomed moment of each week.

Zach required 24/7, one-on-one supervision. Feeding him involved monitoring every bite of food or sip of liquid he put into his mouth and dealing with occasional terrifying choking episodes. We needed to take him to the bathroom every two hours—day and night—and deal with accidents whenever and wherever they happened. His newfound ability to walk—but inability to balance—necessitated staying close to him every moment.

Sleeping with him for his safety meant getting up numerous times every night to take him to the bathroom, holding him down when he wanted to get out of bed, or getting bear-hugged in the middle of the night when he happily realized he was not alone.

By Sunday evening, I was no longer intoxicated at the sight of him but hungover from physical, mental, and emotional exhaustion.

As for Zach, it was clear all he wanted was to be home. When his school van pulled up to our house on Fridays, I had to sprint around the van to get to him before he tried to get out on his own. But when we pulled into the long driveway of the group home on Sunday nights, Zach always closed his eyes, shook his head, and then let it fall back onto the headrest of the car before he slumped forward into a limp prayer posture.

When I got out of the car, Zach stayed put. I'd slowly walk around and open his door. But Zach remained seated. "Come on, Zach," I whispered in his ear as I bent over and released his seat belt. Face down and eyes pressed closed, he shook his head with a defiant, "No."

We knew he was treated well here. Zach had few words, few ways of expressing his disappointment that our time together was over for another five days. But his body language made it clear.

Eventually, I'd prevail and would walk him inside, give him a long hug, and tap out—*off duty*—with a sigh. Relieved but distraught. Many a Sunday night as I drove away from Zach's residence, the road swam in front of me. This was not the dorm I'd imagined driving away from after saying good-bye to a soon-to-be eighteen-year-old son.

Letting go of my dreams and expectations for Zach's life tortured me. I rarely let Tammy see that side. She carried a larger share of the grief, as if we were two people hauling a heavy load but she had to walk backward. Same load. Different methods of maneuvering. Maybe if I'd let her see my heartbroken side more often . . .

Yes, I was tortured. But other than the prolonged good-byes, Zach showed no remorse over his new situation. My vain imagining that Zach moped around his new home after I left, devastated that I was gone, was shattered a few months into the transition.

I pretended to leave but then hid and watched how Zach behaved once I was out of the picture. Within seconds—five at most—he engaged anyone within eyeshot. And everyone within reach soon found themselves drawn into his company by the gravitational pull of his enthusiasm and joy—and usually his embrace.

I soon learned that the forlorn look on his face when I left was not the expression of a son who became miserable the moment I was gone. It was instead one more way Zach communicated his love for me. It seemed to flow from an endless reservoir of affection he also possessed for others.

Tammy

I couldn't begin to explain to Pat how distressing it was for me to have Zach with us all weekend long, in spite of how much I wanted him home. Those two days at the end of a busy week once meant simple meals and relaxation. Now every minute was filled with Zach's protection, care, or cleanup.

What kind of mother wouldn't want her son to be home as long as possible? But all the complications in our family life intensified on Fridays. Nate and Soren had once lived for Saturdays and Sundays after a long week of school. Our second-floor apartment was no longer a place to crash. It was a makeshift rehab facility with one very needy patient. The one-on-one time we'd managed to grab with the boys was gone now that their brother's equipment, needs, and voice filled the apartment the entire weekend.

Life was harder with Zach home. I could hardly argue with Nate or Soren when they asked, "Does it have to be *every* weekend, *all* weekend?" I asked myself the same question. So much time and energy were spent caring for Zach rather than enjoying him on the weekends. He couldn't be left unsupervised for a second.

Pat, though growing wearier with every visit, seemed to be in his element. He wanted to be with Zach all the time. It worried me, as if Zach had become Pat's sole reason for living, his oxygen tank.

But my reasons for stressing out during Zach's home visits went deeper than the increased workload and the complications that upset the tenuous balance I worked so hard to maintain.

When he crossed the threshold of home after his injury, we kissed and hugged, glad to see each other. But almost immediately, sadness descended as I considered all we had lost.

The first Sunday Zach was with us in our apartment, Pat brought him into the room with my reading chair, my private sanctuary. Pat guided Zach to my chair. I knelt beside my son, looking for the glint in his eye that had marked so many special moments of our togetherness time before his injury. It was there. My heart leapt. He hadn't sung since that miracle moment in the hospital so long ago. I hadn't heard his clear voice, a voice so often filled with tenderness toward me.

Was he on the verge of another breakthrough? Would this setting—this sweet sanctuary—witness the unleashing of what had remained locked in the prison of Zach's mind? Would he sing to me? Affirm me?

His mouth began to move.

Say it, Zach! Say it.

I knew that look. I knew the glimmer.

Zach laughed over his inability to push the words out of his mouth.

It wasn't funny. *Zach, say it! Say something.*

In a fleeting moment, the glint vanished. His eyes had been locked on mine, but now looked upward and to his right. Confusion masked his face.

My heart sank twice as far as it had risen. While trying to form the idea of what he'd wanted to say, his brain had gotten stuck. He'd forgotten what he was thinking.

I rested my head in his lap and moaned. The longing—so palpable, so intense—to hear my son's voice consumed me. When I lifted my head to look at him, his face was contorted, bewildered. He had no idea what he'd done to upset me. That much was good. I could almost hear his internal thoughts and wished I could.

What did I do to Peach? Why is she crying?

I didn't know if I could bear that level of pain every weekend. But I would rarely see my son if I didn't.

Though Zach couldn't communicate with words, he continued to influence me and my faith. On Mother's Day in 2009—just a few months after his move to the May Center School—I posted this update on Zach's CaringBridge site, describing a poignant moment one weekend when my patience had worn thin:

> The arduous process of getting Zach ready for the day began: helping him eat so he didn't choke, shower so he didn't fall, brush his teeth thoroughly, comb his hair, take his medications, and dress. An hour later I rushed helping him into his socks, leg brace, and shoes. We were already running late for an event.
>
> I put the brace on Zach's right foot and tried to shove the brace into his shoe but failed several times and grew impatient. He gently placed his hand on my shoulder. I knew he wanted me to look up at him, but I resisted. Eventually, I looked into his eyes. Noncondemning yet beckoning, he called me out of impatience into love.
>
> I melted onto the floor, confessed my impatience to Zach and to God, and asked Him for the strength to continue the task. Zach's sad and gentle gaze helped me visualize how God looks at me when I sin, not with condemnation but with sorrow, imploring me to live according to His ways.

Pat

Though Zach was almost completely nonverbal, he somehow broke through the barriers to minister to other nonverbal residents at the May Center. Especially one boy with autism. The house staff marveled at how Zach befriended him and managed to calm him when others could not. Zach. With all his limitations.

When this young man got worked up and out of control, Zach would wave his hand like a magic wand. It calmed the boy. Somehow all the disturbances in the force of this young man's universe were quelled by Zach's presence.

Stepping back into a home for children with disabilities was a strange déjà vu experience for me. I'd tried to keep my memories of the Sizanani Children's Home in South Africa at a safe emotional distance. We'd chosen the May Center for Zach because we felt our son fit well with the impressive staff members, who were athletic, smart, and skilled. As I consider that thought now, it occurs to me that we chose the staff for their resemblance to who Zach had once *been*. Who I hoped he could become again, given enough time and effort. I clung to the perception that this phase was a necessary but temporary next step to getting him back to his old school on his way to a nearly full recovery.

But occasionally, the circumstances of this new routine broke through with brute force. The school was in many ways an American version of what we'd experienced in South Africa at the children's home. Zach struggled in ways the other residents did. He fit in.

I could no longer maintain a singular focus on Zach's full recovery and found myself wrestling with the possibility that the summer preceding Zach's injury had set us up to dive into a story that was heading in a different direction than any of us wanted to go.

I fought off the memory of my son's voice—strong and articulate at the time, just a few days before his injury—telling me,

"I wonder if God would ever have me become like one of them."

Months after Zach arrived at the rehab school, we received an invitation to their annual signature event, the May Center School Talent Show. Tammy needed to attend Nate's report card night at his school, but Soren and I made the drive and arrived just in time for the event.

We'd attended a similar talent show on our last night at the South African home for children with disabilities. In South Africa, each member of our American team had formed at least one strong friendship with a child in the home. Some, like Zach, had many special friends. Both Zach and I had become particularly close to a seventeen-year-old boy with autism named JJ.

On the night of the talent show in Sizanani, JJ staked out his spot in the center of the front row. When he saw me, he nervously glanced back and forth between me and the one empty seat adjacent to him. I took that as a sign that he wanted me to sit next to him.

Is that what he wanted? Was the seat reserved for someone else? Maybe the chair had been vacated because the not-so-pleasant smell surrounding JJ indicated he was overdue for a diaper change. After greeting him, I moved to the back of the room to sit with the rest of my family.

The South African staff, dressed in beautifully colored African attire, kicked off the festivities with a native Zulu dance. Some of our American students followed with a few of their favorite party tricks. One of the children's home's residents—Thabiso—wowed the crowd with his amazing wheelchair stunts.

At some point, a familiar smell alerted me. JJ had migrated

from his front-row seat to stand directly behind our family in the back row. We invited him to sit with us. In classic JJ style, without establishing any eye contact, moving his head in every possible direction—except to look directly at me—he eventually sat down in the seat next to us.

The final performers of the night were the McLeod family, in what I'd assumed would be the most underwhelming act. Zach would strum his guitar as we sang a mellow worship song he had taught us, a song we'd rehearsed only once before the talent show.

Tammy got us started on beat and on key. But it soon became clear that something that transcended our singing was beginning to happen. The room became electric with energy.

Eventually I figured out the real reason for the mounting liveliness in the crowd. JJ was once again on the move. He had made his way from where we'd left him in the back to the front of the room. He turned his back to the audience—as if doing so would make him invisible—and sidestepped closer and closer to our family as we sang.

His head swiveling in every direction, he clapped his hands and almost simultaneously stomped his foot, neither of which were quite on beat.

Once JJ made his way to the very center of our family, the audience became unglued. JJ faced Zach and reached to strum his guitar. Without hesitation, Zach raised his strumming hand in the air. JJ took over strumming with the exuberance of a rock star. The place erupted with applause. The evening ended on a perfect note.

That scene was on my mind as Soren and I heard the strikingly similar noise of enthusiastic students and school staff gathered for the celebration at the May Center School half a world away.

The déjà vu continued when we stepped inside and scanned the room for Zach. We found him—just as we had found JJ on that last night in South Africa—in the very center seat of the front row. Soren and I greeted him, then settled into the back row—the only available seats in the auditorium.

Zach's was the first hand to go up and the first voice to cry out when a classmate was introduced or when an act came to an end. If not for the staff member sitting next to him holding him down, everyone would have received a standing ovation.

Whatever somber feelings I had about walking into a room filled with children with disabilities, knowing my own son was among them, were overcome by the realization that Zach was not throwing any pity party for himself. He was the happiest person there.

The unbridled joy of the children, the guileless way every single one performed and cheered for one another, the astonishing abilities of those challenged by stupefying disabilities triggered flashback after flashback of the children's home in South Africa. For the next two hours, my mind flitted back and forth between continents.

When the curtain opened for the final act, Zach was sitting center stage with a guitar strap around his neck. The auditorium exploded with cheers. Seated behind and to the side of Zach was the May Center School staff person who worked most closely with him—Kiley, who was a budding musician at the time. When she'd learned that Zach loved music and played the guitar before his injury, she took it upon herself to help him relearn the guitar.

Somehow, despite his brain injury, Zach's long-term memory of the songs he used to play before his injury remained intact. Likewise, the agility in his left hand, the one he used to press down the strings to make a chord, still worked well. But he no longer had the motor control to make his right hand strum. That's where Kiley stepped in.

Zach grabbed the neck of his guitar with his left hand. Gracefully and gently, Kiley leaned over Zach's shoulder and began to strum the guitar. Once again, with the help of a friend, Zach filled a room with music—but not just any music. Together, Kiley and Zach played the same song Zach had taught us the night we sang together in the South African talent show.

The roles had shifted, but the music produced the same effect. Just as Zach had done with JJ, Kiley helped Zach meld two worlds together, smudging the lines between ability and disability, and filling a room with cheers and weeping as they played a worship song with these lyrics:

> Your will above all else
> My purpose remains
> The art of losing myself in bringing You praise
> Everlasting, Your light will shine when all else fades
> Never ending, Your glory goes beyond all fame
> And the cry of my heart is to bring You praise
> From the inside out
> Lord, my soul cries out

CHAPTER

10

Pat

A new football season neared. A season with scars and bandaged memories.

Tammy stood in the doorway of my home office one night after dinner. I'd cooked a favorite Thai dish we all enjoyed. She'd done the dishes, her preferred role. That allowed me time to prep for my next day's presentation.

"Soren and I had a talk," she said, leaning her back against the doorjamb. "He talked, I should say."

"About what?"

Tammy hesitated. "He made one statement, Pat. Last night when I tucked him into bed and prayed for him, he blurted, 'I can't believe you're letting me play football.'"

Not play football? The kid was a natural. "What did you tell him?"

I said, "We're not."

"No pushback from him?"

"None."

Even though Soren showed signs of being better at the game than anyone else in our family, his comment made it clear he was no longer all in when it came to the sport that—from his perspective—wrecked the life of the brother he'd idolized.

"That's it then?"

Tammy stepped away from the doorjamb. "Are you going to try to talk him back into playing?"

"No. I can't do that."

In some respects, a year after Zach's injury, we were no longer a football family.

We settled into a new rhythm—living without Zach during the week and having him at home with us on weekends. With Chelsea back at college after summer break, Nate now a freshman in high school, and Soren an active preteen, we continued to bounce among their needs and interests while caring for Zach.

Chelsea had survived her freshman year at college, despite the turmoil at home and her having to experience it long distance. With Zach "stable," she'd started a new school year with less trauma weighing her down. She'd spent the summer working at a Christian camp. New friends there listened to her stories of what had happened with Zach and the family, offering the support she needed, the focused attention and listening ears any young woman would crave.

Nate acted in theater productions, rowed crew, and sang in a select a cappella group. As an honors student, he began making plans for his own fast-approaching college days.

∞

A year to the day after the call that changed everything, I was back in the same auditorium at the same event, welcoming college students to a new school year.

Our Friday night large-group meetings coincided with Zach's arrival home from his school, so we decided to take him with us. Only two times in the twenty years of that citywide gathering had it been held in that particular auditorium rather than on the Harvard campus. Two times—the year when I got the call about Zach and this night, one year later.

So when I walked Zach into the building, flashbacks pierced me like sniper shots. I felt like I was the one who was concussed. Everything happening around me felt like it had already happened and as if I were watching it through a fogged window, not really present.

At the end of the program, the leader of the musical group invited everyone to stand and join in singing closing worship songs. Before we could make our way to our seats, one of our staff members ran toward us.

When Zach saw her, his face lit up. He knew her well and hugged her hard, in a way that made it clear he had no intention of letting go.

It was Faith, the woman who the year before had lived on the third floor of our multifunction house. Faith was the only person other than Nate who was home on the night of Zach's accident. When Nate couldn't reach us on our phones, he'd found her. Faith had figured out a way to contact us when we weren't answering our phones, which were tucked away in our backpacks, silenced so they wouldn't interrupt the meeting. She'd called Julia, who she knew was at the meeting. Julia had handed her phone to me so Nate could tell me what had happened.

Once Zach finally let go of his hold on Faith, I told her, "I know this is hard to believe, but right now I'm standing in the exact spot where I stood when Julia gave me her phone." Exactly one year earlier.

On this night, Faith hadn't been looking for us when we bumped into each other. She'd been on her way to the foyer to help students sign up for a Boston harbor cruise.

Zach quickly checked out of our ongoing conversation and listened to the music. Faith and I continued to marvel over the coincidence of our meeting at that exact place on that particular day.

Suddenly, Zach shocked us both by busting out singing the lyrics to the song that the band was playing. I had never heard him sing as loud nor as clear as he sang at that moment. Even more shocking was the song he sang.

Faith and I looked at each other, awestruck, the coincidence hitting us simultaneously. We both knew the backstory of the song. A father had lost four daughters in a shipwreck. Just days after their ship sank in the Atlantic, the father—Horatio Spafford—boarded a vessel so he could reunite with his wife who alone had survived. At one point, the ship's captain called Spafford to his cabin to tell him that their vessel was passing over the exact spot where the ship had gone down, claiming the lives of his daughters. He returned to his cabin and wrote the lyrics to the song that Zach was now so enthusiastically and spontaneously belting out—"It is well, it is well with my soul."

When the song ended, we hugged and said good-bye. Faith, the staff member in charge of the boat cruise event, was wearing—of all things—a captain's hat.

Tammy

Pat and I had grown accustomed to friends and family starting nearly every conversation with, "How's Zach doing?" Knowing people cared was both sustaining and draining. "He's the same—totally happy and joyful . . . and severely disabled" was my frequent but uncomfortable answer. Whenever there *was* an update to report, we found ourselves repeating the information until we grew hoarse from keeping people informed.

Once in a while, a friend would ask a different question: "How are *you* doing?"

That was the question that always brought tears to my eyes. It validated our pain and acknowledged that Zach wasn't the only one battling to recover. It allowed me the freedom to speak the truth about the hardships, fatigue, and sadness that shadowed our lives. It gave me opportunity to be honest about Zach's prognosis.

But Pat often stepped in as soon as I responded and offered a counterpoint—a differing view that always brought Zach's "progress" back to the focus of the conversation. He seemed to thrive on the question "How's Zach doing?"—which he took as an invitation to tell stories about his son.

"You should have seen what Zach did in the elevator the other day," Pat would tell people. "You know how most of us get in an elevator and immediately turn to look at the numbers scrolling over the doors? Not Zach. He stepped in and refused to turn around. Instead he tried to establish eye contact with everyone, smiling, waving, giving high fives and bear hugs to anyone who would let him. I've never seen so many smiles on an elevator in my life."

As Zach's mom, I was apparently the only one not smiling.

One night at a meal with friends, I reached a tipping point. Our friends asked honest questions and wanted honest answers.

"So, any changes with Zach?"

Any miracles? No. Measurable progress? Not unless progress can be measured under a magnifying glass.

Pat was busting with pride and the latest stories. "He did the funniest thing the other day when he couldn't form the word he was looking for at my birthday party, so he—"

"Pat. Not that story. We're eating."

"It's okay," our friends said, glancing at each other as if they might need to play peacemakers.

Apparently unaware of my increasingly tensed shoulder muscles, Pat launched deeper into the story. "His friend Kat and others were giving minispeeches to wish me a happy birthday. Kat encouraged Zach to say something too."

Pat grinned like a father potty training an inventive toddler. "We later found out he was trying to say, 'My . . . dad . . . snores . . . but . . . I . . . love . . . him.'"

Our friends chuckled.

"He said the word *snores* and then got stuck. His mouth tried to form that next word. It wouldn't come. So he pointed to his butt. His version of sign language."

Pat's laughter rang for a moment. Our friends smiled, but

stopped when they noticed I didn't find it funny. I'd found it hilarious when it first happened. But not tonight. What Pat thought so delightful was rooted in our son's inability to speak a simple word.

I was quiet the rest of the night—emotionally withdrawn—seething as Pat continued with clever anecdotes about our brain-damaged son.

Pat was equally livid when we got to the car. "You make it sound as if Zach is dead, Tammy." He slid the key into the ignition but then gripped the wheel instead of starting the engine.

"Why do you have such a hard time admitting that what's happened is excruciating?" My throat tightened. We rarely raised our voices with each other, but this was too much. "You make me feel as though I'm not only wrong, but somehow less spiritual because I acknowledge and am not afraid to talk about what we've lost, what *Zach* has lost!"

Pat stared at me and sighed. "Why do you have such a hard time seeing all the good that's coming out of this, the joy he's still bringing to everyone he meets? He's still here, Tammy." His voice softened. "He's still here."

"I do see the good coming out of this," I told him, eyes locked onto his gaze. "I have pages and pages in my journal about what I am thankful for, what I'm learning through this trial, what I'm learning from Zach, how God is using Zach in others' lives . . . And yes, he is here. But he is also not here."

I accused Pat of fixating on what we had. He accused me of fixating on what we'd lost.

And both were true. Inescapable. Impossible to resolve. A loss like ours could be brutal on a marriage. The moment passed. The differences didn't.

∞

Sometimes—rarely—Pat and I would be asked, "How are the *two of you* doing?"

"You mean, us? The *marriage* part of us?"

One day, my answer must have been unfiltered. The listening friend not only suggested we make regular counseling appointments part of our biweekly schedule, but she also insisted on paying for them.

I hope she understands the value of that gift. Because *I* process verbally, a regular appointment for counseling held high appeal. Pat didn't resist, but I could tell he internally calculated the miles and hours it might take him away from Zach.

Both of us soon found that counseling gave us breathing space, a safe place to talk. We gained tips for keeping our disagreements from escalating and acknowledged our mutually shared core truths of underlying concern for and high respect for each other. But it seemed nothing could reverse our views that so often pulled me toward the losses and Pat toward the gains.

What thoughts might have entered our minds or our conversations if we hadn't already settled the issue of lifetime commitment to each other? A nonnegotiable. Our situation—consuming as it was—couldn't erode our foundational commitment. We were both determined—and united—on that important point.

My acute sense of loss faced additional challenges because of the work we did every day. Discovering that link didn't make it easier, but it made sense. Pat's and my careers dictated heavy involvement in the vital, vibrant lives of Harvard students, young people Zach's age, accomplishing things Zach would never accomplish. Learning. Dating. News of the grad schools they were getting into. Mapping career paths. Finding life-mates. Watching for service opportunities. Traveling. Graduating. Building homes and families of their own. The young people I'd been assigned to serve were constant reminders of what was now unattainable for Zach. I dodged darts of emotional pain over their unlimited potential.

Because nobody from the admissions offices knew anything about Zach's injury, college flyers flooded our mailbox even a year after his injury, when he would have been making campus visits and starting the application process. The symbolism of those "you have a great future ahead of you" flyers stung. Our friends were talking about where their kids were applying to college. Zach's friends were moving on. He was left behind.

When we look back at what we've come through, we often recognize moments that held more significance than we realized. Now, as I recalled the pain of the college flyers that never seemed to stop coming, I remembered too how hard it had been a month after Zach's injury to call the college tutoring center to tell them what had happened and let them know he wouldn't—not then, at least—continue preparing for college. During that phone call, I could barely speak the sentences. Even that early in Zach's recovery journey, it seemed to put a stamp of finality on what I prayed was a temporary delay in his and our plans. I hadn't known at the time, but it was another dream forever altered.

When I crossed paths with Zach's high school friends, I fought jealousy over the vast horizons still open to them, the plans they were making, their creative minds, even the fact that they could remember what happened three minutes earlier.

Unlike my son.

11

Tammy

Time wore on. It *wore* on. Sameness interrupted by minor skirmishes with infections or pneumonia. Everything—everything—complicated by the brain injury.

How had a year and a half passed now since our life was turned upside down? How had Pat and I managed to keep navigating unsettled, churning waters without tossing the other person overboard?

When he and Zach snuggled together on our couch to watch football, what should have been a warm scene disgusted me. I was probably a little envious of the camaraderie they had that didn't include me.

My overriding emotion, however, was anger at the game of

football and what it could do to a young brain. I excused Zach's infatuation with the game that hadn't quite ended his life but had certainly mangled it. His brain processes no longer followed a smooth, logical path.

But how could Pat derive pleasure from the sport that kept me on the edge of anger? From wherever I was in the house, I'd hear the NFL commentators' voices during pregame on Sundays and could feel my blood pressure rising.

"Hey, Zach, game's about to start," Pat would say. "I'll get us something to drink. Don't move."

I'd glance at the players—suited up, supposedly protected by their gear and helmets—and wonder how their wives or moms would feel if the player they loved got one concussion too many. If this were the last game they'd ever play. If years from now, as newscasters reported, these same men developed CTE—chronic traumatic encephalopathy, a neurodegenerative disease found in people who've had multiple head injuries. If their future would be marred by premature dementia, brain dysfunction, personality changes, depression, criminal behavior, even suicidal thoughts because of a career of football's hard hits.

Even from the kitchen or bedroom, I could hear that play after play was punctuated with Zach's grunts and screeches, as well as the slaps of a stream of high fives he and Pat shared when the teams made progress on the field.

Did I harbor resentment that Zach and Pat now shared a closeness over football that Zach and I had once shared in song and prayer and tender moments of deep conversation, conversations we would never have in the same way again? Maybe. But my overriding emotion at the time was the absurdity of watching a potential train wreck and calling it "sport."

During what little football I could stand to watch anymore, I held my breath, anticipating a moment when a player's head would hit the turf, or a helmet would crash against an opponent's helmet hard enough to scramble an egg.

It happened all too often. It had happened during the Super Bowl one year. More than one. But one I clearly recall.

He's not moving. I remember the sinking feeling in my stomach after watching the player go down. Even Zach had held his breath when the pro football player—in a game watched by millions of people around the world—lay motionless on the turf.

The scene that had been deafeningly loud moments earlier grew funeral-home quiet on the screen. Sixty-eight thousand people can create a new definition of cacophony. In an instant, they collectively swallowed their noise and trained their attention on the still body on the 40-yard line.

He's not moving. Move!

Team trainers and referees encircled the figure while the crack of the helmet-to-helmet collision replayed on the Jumbotron and on fifty-two-inch TV screens in homes from Boston to Belize to Bora Bora. Commentators theorized about what kind of penalty the defensive player would incur for the hard hit. Fifteen yards for unnecessary roughness? Ejection from the game?

No. No flag. No penalty.

The player who'd made the tackle hadn't met the requirements for an unnecessary roughness ejection because his opponent had established possession of the ball after a pass and was no longer considered "completely defenseless."

A brutal, vicious, but legal blow, the commentators said.

Brutal. Vicious. But legal. Even the sports reporters seemed to have trouble forming the words.

A twitch or voluntary movement? What was that?

The player sat, then was gingerly helped to his feet. Rocked, stunned, concussed, he staggered from the field and was immediately escorted to the locker room. No sit-on-the-bench-until-you-catch-your-breath evaluation. The decision had already been made: He would see no more of the biggest game of the year, and possibly the biggest of his career.

The empathetic but excitement-hungry crowd—both in the stadium and around the world—returned their attention to the game.

It looks like he's going to be okay, a sports announcer theorized. *What a relief to see him moving and now walking off the field under his own power. But what a huge disappointment that he must be forced out of the biggest game of his life. The next play is underway. Let's get this game back on track. So much is at stake.*

A quick update from the sports announcer outside the locker room assuaged any remaining crumbs of spectator concern. The game played on.

It played to its confetti-strewn conclusion for all but the family of the injured player—and other families whose loved ones have been through concussion protocol, with varying results.

For one shaken family watching in Boston—*our* family— scenes like that were reminders of how our lives had been changed forever by a hard hit.

The game doesn't "play on" when the motionless body on the field is your sixteen-year-old son.

I forced my mind to stop replaying the horrible hit that

Super Bowl Sunday and looked at Zach and Pat now. They were in full spectator mode—cheering and snacking as if a young man's future hadn't been rewritten by a single hit.

"How can you still enjoy watching that stupid game?"

Pat may have never heard my voice that harsh. Ever. His eyes wide, he looked at Zach, crowded close to him on the couch.

I stopped with my one-sentence rant, not because of the shocked look on Pat's face, but because of the sorrow on Zach's. I stormed back to my study, sat in my reading chair, and flooded Pat's inbox with articles on sports-related brain injuries.

I'm not sure what pushed me over the edge that day. It may have been all the articles I had read about other fallen football players, or reverberations from the upsetting interaction I'd had with a brain scientist about second impact syndrome when Zach was still in Spaulding Rehab Hospital. He'd said if someone has one concussion and then another before the first is fully healed, catastrophic head injuries with massive swelling may result. Some people die from it. Some suffer permanent severe disability.

Had we missed signs of an earlier hit, a previous concussion? When Zach had asked for aspirin for his headache earlier in the week before his life-altering injury, was that for more than an ordinary headache?

Was something already brewing in the days before the scrimmage that ended his sports career and changed us all?

Sometime in those hazy months after Zach's injury, a football dad (we never did find out who) told my mom that on the bus ride to the last scrimmage in which Zach would ever play, he had asked the man's son, "What does it feel like to have a concussion?"

We didn't know about that conversation. I'd handed him the bottle of aspirin when he'd asked. I found three in the bottom of his backpack when it was returned to us. But he hadn't told me that the word *concussion* was on his mind. I thought he had a regular headache.

After the accident, Pat told me that two days before his injury, Zach approached him and said he had a headache. He didn't feel like eating and just wanted to go to bed. Pat asked him, "Did you get dinged? Did you have a hard hit that rattled you or made you see stars?" The answers were all no.

Knowing what we do now, both Pat and I would have pressed to find out more about what was going on and then taken Zach to a doctor. At the time, Pat concluded Zach was dehydrated from two hard practices on one of the hottest days of the summer.

Over time, my heart had become irreversibly hardened toward the game I once loved to watch. I resented it. Pat had become the victim of my resentment that Sunday.

Later that night, after their game ended and he'd driven Zach back to his residential home, Pat walked into our room.

"What was that all about?" he asked, scowling.

"What was *what* about?"

He pointed over his shoulder toward the family room. "Your comment about my watching that 'stupid' game of football."

"What about it?" I said, determined to hold my ground.

"Well, that's an insulting thing to say. It feels like a pretty strong indictment on my character." He tapped his chest with the palm of his hand.

"I honestly can't believe you still watch that game," I said.

Pat crossed his arms. "Tammy, what happened to Zach was a fluke. Why can't you accept that?"

"It's not a fluke. Read the emails I just sent you." I reframed my growing frustration into a plea. "Pat, you know football trashes brains."

"And *you* know that giving a kid a football helmet is a lot safer than handing him the keys to a car." The veins in Pat's temples throbbed visibly.

"That's a stinking lousy comparison," I said, anger boiling again. "Kids need to learn to drive, but they don't *have* to play football."

"I would much rather have my kids on a football field after school, conditioning their bodies, than behind the wheel of a car, messing around with their friends."

"Football isn't the only sport that conditions bodies." I fought to keep my voice even. "Young people can choose a different sport that doesn't mangle their brains."

"You know when you say that, you're talking to someone who is a product of that game. A lot of who I am was formed by that 'stupid' game."

I hadn't intended to say it, but how could I not? "Pat, you've had more concussions than anyone I've ever known. You're probably going to end up with CTE yourself."

My words hung in the air as if electrified. Pat didn't respond.

"Pat, you're part of the football culture." I walked to where he stood. "I'm not sure anyone inside of it can see this issue clearly."

"Says the person who once admitted that one of her guilty pleasures in life was watching hard hits in football."

His words cut me, giving an even sharper edge to the guilt

that lived inside me. How many tears would this pain cost me? I pulled back several feet and leveled my gaze at him. "That was before I knew about the long-term effects of those kinds of hits. Arms and legs heal. Brains don't."

"I get it, Tammy. Every game has risks. Football isn't the only sport with a concussion and CTE problem. But you know as well as I do that *not* playing *any* games has its own risks to a person's long-term health."

"I'm not arguing that point." I sighed. "All I know is I'm done with it. Football is not worth losing a son."

"We didn't lose a son, Tammy."

"We lost his potential. You can't deny that."

We both fell silent at the truth.

Pat

Almost two years. Tammy and I kept functioning. Forgiving when we needed to.

Zach was no longer making measurable progress. His recovery leveled off. He could see, but only what was to the left of the center of his focus; nothing on the right registered in his brain. He could walk, but he needed a brace on his right leg and someone close by to steady him if he lost his balance. He could move his right hand, but not in a controlled way and not enough to strum a guitar. He could eat soft food, but required close supervision to keep him from stuffing his mouth or choking. He could remember his life before the injury, but not what happened five minutes earlier. He could immediately comprehend and respond nonverbally to what someone said to him, but struggled to utter a single word, let alone a full sentence.

Though he was far from fully recovered, we received hope that buoyed us. Zach was deemed well enough to do what he had set his heart to do since the moment he found a way to communicate with us. He was emotionally ready and physically okayed to go back to South Africa and continue the work he'd started—caring for the most vulnerable.

Many rallied around Zach's "Don't go back to Africa without me" plea. His school sponsored a second annual 3-on-3 basketball tournament fund-raiser. Other friends raised money by collecting pledges and then completing the Boston Marathon. Together, they donated more than enough to pay for Zach's return to South Africa and for a 24/7 helper to accompany him.

The Sizanani Children's Home could not provide housing for us that summer. So we traveled ahead of Zach in order to settle into a new and unknown living arrangement and to get the service learning project—the Mamelodi Initiative—functioning before he arrived. Zach would then join us when we had the capacity to care for his needs and keep him safe.

Kat, one of Zach's closest friends and Marty's daughter, volunteered to accompany him to South Africa the week after we landed. Kat had known Zach his entire life—from babysitting him when we lived in Montana to living with us and working as part of the student ministries team. No doctor, teacher, therapist, or family member could pull more out of Zach than Kat. She may not have had a degree in medicine, but she was an expert on our son. While therapists tried to get Zach talking, Kat got him laughing. While nurses helped him walk again, Kat had him making others laugh again. While doctors worked on his vision, Kat got him winking, and while teachers focused on testing, Kat got him teasing people. She got him to be himself, if only for a moment.

As predicted, the flight to South Africa was exhausting—for both Kat and Zach. For someone like Zach, still struggling with sleep, swallowing, balance, and continence issues, everything had gone amazingly well—until the second leg of the trip.

Partway through the flight, Zach indicated that he needed to go to the bathroom. Kat walked him to the lavatory and through the closed door kept asking if everything was okay. After a few minutes, Zach stopped responding. Kat tried to open the door, but Zach had locked it. She raised her voice. Still no response. She raised it a little higher, but to no avail. She tried knocking. Nothing. She knocked louder. Still no response.

On the edge of panic, Kat notified the flight attendants. They also tried to get Zach to respond or to unlock the door, without success. Finally, they retrieved a tool to break into the lavatory. To their relief, they found Zach sitting peacefully on the toilet with his head bowed and hands clasped in a praying posture.

"Zach!" Kat blurted in exasperation. Without opening his eyes or lifting his head, he simply raised his left-hand index finger to signal—as he had countless times before—"Excuse me. I'm praying. Give me a minute."

The flight attendants reportedly tried in vain to stifle their laughter. Kat found it less humorous.

When they finally arrived, nothing could hold Zach back. He soaked up every minute on the rust-colored soil of South

Africa. Wherever he went, he left a trail of smiling people behind him.

We spent most of our time with the children in the township of Mamelodi. Near the end of Zach's stay we slipped away from our work in the township to visit the children's home.

The one-hour drive from our new home base to the children's home at Sizanani was a quiet ride. Memories made me pensive and melancholy. Tammy expressed her own apprehension. We had been looking forward to this day for so long that it never occurred to me that it would be anything other than a joyful, celebratory reunion.

But the closer we got to Sizanani, the more I realized that the happiest memories of the summer before Zach's injury were the most difficult to ponder. Visions of Zach as he was before ran through my mind—playing the guitar, kicking soccer balls, and carrying two or three children at a time in the orphanage.

We stepped out of the car and explored the Sizanani property.

Heavy sadness smothered me as we walked across the field where Zach had run pass patterns and caught footballs that summer two years earlier. The memory of timing him in his 40-yard dash in preparation for the coming football season threatened to bring me to my knees. Nearly all my last memories of Zach's athletic and musical abilities had happened on these grounds.

As I rounded every corner, a new and pain-shrouded memory flashed across my mind. The thought that Zach would likely never marry, play football, lead worship, or drive a car again made for a somber walk across Sizanani.

"Dad, come on," Nate said, breaking me out of my stupor. "Let's go see the kids." He bounced with excitement.

Nate and Soren led the way as Tammy, Zach, and I walked toward the children with disabilities, children like my son. The jarring sensory overload, which years earlier had jolted me into a sober state, jolted me out of it again. As Zach limped alongside me into the courtyard, the children gathered around him and the rest of our family. Some of them recognized us. Others did not but were glad to see us anyway. As expected, the infamous JJ kept his distance but slowly warmed up to us as we hugged, laughed, and played with the other children.

Zach was just as gentle, happy, humble, kind, and effective at engaging these children as he had been before. I watched Zach connect the worlds of "ability" and "disability" again.

At the end of our day at Sizanani, as we said good-bye to the children and made our way to the car, we passed a wooden sign with a Zulu word carved into it, a sign that hung over the entrance to the children's home. It triggered one last, comforting memory.

Two years earlier, when we'd loaded up to leave Sizanani, one of our teammates made an impression of that sign to take back to America with her. Grabbing supplies from the children's home, she had laid a piece of white paper over the sign and rubbed charcoal over the letters until a lasting imprint of the word appeared on the paper.

A couple of months after Zach's injury, we'd arrived home from the hospital one night to find a large gift waiting for us with a note from that teammate. It was the rubbing of the sign, matted and framed and ready to be hung in our home. Even though I had seen the sign at Sizanani, I never knew until then what the word meant.

That rubbing now hangs over the entrance to our house

as a perpetual reminder of the force that guides and sustains the Sizanani community, the force that inspired and sustained Zach's determination to get back to Africa, and the force that continues to inspire and comfort us in the face of an indefinable loss.

The Zulu word *THEMBALETHU* engraved into that sign simply means "our hope."

CHAPTER

12

Tammy

Taking Zach back to Africa was the fulfillment of a dream. But it was also a nightmare. It underscored how complicated our lives had become. Now Zach was not racing into adulthood at full steam. He needed constant, 24/7 monitoring and help with the simplest tasks. The complexities of our family life showed no promise of resolving.

After we returned to our stateside routine and prepared for yet another start to a new school year, the history-rich monastery I jogged past during my runs along the river continued to serve as a place of refuge for me: stone, subdued light, silence. The white marble sculpture of baby Jesus with His outstretched hand welcomed me each time I entered through the carved black walnut doors. Seeing His mother, the Virgin Mary, holding Him reminded me that she also lost a son, and I felt her vicarious empathy for my loss.

When I stopped there once a month the first year, and once every few months after that, I would sit in silence for a long time, read Scripture, and pray. Sometimes I was moved to light candles for my family—one for each child, one for Pat, and one for myself. It wasn't part of our church tradition. But during these visits to that quiet, sacred place, it was meaningful to my healing, my faith, my hope.

One day after my run and an especially meaningful time in the monastery, I met Pat for our weekly date, this time at the gym we frequented, which happened to be right next to the monastery. We sat around the pool with light streaming in from three sides of plate glass windows and no one else in the pool room. Just us.

As I talked about my experience of connecting with a litany of losses minutes earlier, there at poolside, in a starkly different beauty from the sanctuary from which I'd come, a deluge of sorrow poured out of me.

Pat didn't counter. He didn't try to solve any of the issues or minimize my distress. He simply listened. He let me express my sadness without trying to shield me from it. There my heart cried out what had become clearly defined. That litany of losses, rather than a single loss.

"My mind constantly drifts to Zach. Many times a day. Dinner is hard because I'm distracted by his empty chair. After dinner, when Zach and I washed dishes together, we had so many meaningful conversations about God—lessons we were learning and questions we were processing."

PAT & TAMMY MCLEOD

I paused, wondering if Pat would say something. He didn't. His eyes showed he was taking in my words with no intent of interrupting.

That day, I needed no other invitation to keep pouring it out. "You know how much I've always enjoyed playing basketball with Soren."

Pat said nothing. He was listening, giving me the *gift* of listening.

"Now it's heartbreaking to me. Zach so loved teaching Soren his moves. That's over too." I swiped at all-too-familiar tears.

Nothing in Pat's expression told me he was growing restless or tired of my deluge, so I kept adding to my list of losses.

"Zach used to be so involved in Nate's and Soren's lives. That will never happen again. Never. I ache for them. I know they miss their brother, but it's so hard for them to talk about it."

Still no interruption from my husband. What a gift. What a healing, priceless gift.

My chest tightened. "I miss hearing Zach say, 'Good-bye, Peach. I love you' every morning when he left for school. I can almost hear the *echo* of it, but there's a lonely void I can't ignore at the beginning of my day."

Zach seemed everywhere to me . . . and nowhere.

Pat listened. Nothing more.

When I was spent, my sorrow spent, I told Pat I wasn't sure I should grieve those losses. Zach might get better. He might be able to do some of those things again.

Pat said, "I think we should grieve the losses we have now, but not those of the future."

It was wisdom I could absorb because I knew I'd been heard.

∞

Questions about Zach's future continued to plague us. A May Center School staff member told us Zach would need an apartment with a roommate-helper and that our son would require lifelong physical and occupational therapy as well as memory supports. He might be able to manage a simple job, but he wouldn't be able to live alone, go back to school, marry, or have children. We'd heard that before. This time it sank in deeper.

But no one actually knew if more healing were possible. Still the two tensions. Should we search for other treatments that might help him recover more of who he was, or should we accept that what was coming back *had* come back?

In a moment of we're-in-this-together, one of many turning point moments, Pat and I determined to keep searching, keep hoping. But we'd agreed to grieve only *current* losses, not those of the future. Only those directly in front of us.

In all my reading and studying, I discovered memoirs recounting individuals' miraculous recoveries after severe traumatic brain injury. Their stories of the determination, hard work, and sacrifice of others who helped their loved ones regain what they'd lost inspired me. I read voraciously to unearth anything that might help Zach have a strong recovery.

I attended conferences about cutting-edge research in the field. We arranged Zach's schedule so we could try things I had read or heard about: innovative therapies—occupational, physical, speech, water, craniosacral—plus neurofeedback, chiropractic, acupuncture, nutritional supplements, and many types of medications.

Although we spent hundreds of hours trying the same things

as other families, after we passed the second anniversary of his injury, I realized Zach wasn't following the same healing path.

His short-term memory, speech, and his ability to initiate conversation didn't return.

His right arm and leg disability remained unchanged.

I continued to cry out to God for Zach's healing and asked family and friends all over the world to do the same. The prayer that stood out to me most in Scripture was Christ's prayer in the garden of Gethsemane before His crucifixion: "Father, if you are willing, please take this cup of suffering away from me. Yet I want your will to be done, not mine" (Luke 22:42, NLT).

I desperately wanted God to take this cup from me.

How long could I go on writing thousands of emails and making thousands more phone calls to schedule the endless appointments, resolve guardianship issues, stay connected with his caregivers and case managers, get updates from Zach's school and group home, navigate the disability system, speak with social workers, connect with other people who had children or spouses with traumatic brain injury who could recommend additional resources, keep the transportation services informed, rearrange our ministry commitments to accompany Zach to his various appointments, find people who could be with Zach when we couldn't or to take care of Nate and Soren when we couldn't, arrange visits with Zach's friends, keep his teachers and coaches informed and field their offers to help, manage contacts from people who wanted to give money to Zach's special needs trust, update Zach's CaringBridge community posts, order supplies . . . ?

The most difficult part of drinking "the cup" wasn't the work, or the lost sleep, or the many months in hospitals.

Most of all, I missed my son.

∞

Pat asked me what I wanted for my fiftieth birthday. A few years earlier, I'd thought I would celebrate this milestone in a special way. Not now.

Months earlier, Pat and I had planned that during my birthday month we would attend a conference run by a friend of ours. It wasn't a conference where someone speaks and the audience simply listens. Instead, after our friend spoke, we broke into small groups led by licensed clinical Christian counselors.

Ours was a grief group, and over the course of two days, each person had half an hour to share their story without comments from the others. Those in our group had suffered various losses—such as the death of a loved one, divorce, job loss, loss of a home, or estrangement from extended family. Hearing their stories validated our own painful experiences of grief and loss. God had met others in their pain, compelling Pat and me to relate how He had done the same for us. His presence had been revealed through graces large and small. We were able to safely share our feelings and grieve what would never be.

We were honest with the group. We said that though God met us in our pain, Pat and I had grieved in different ways and on different timetables and were rarely in sync, which led to frustration and irritation in our marriage. We functioned. We remained committed to each other. But how was it that we felt so disconnected when permanently connected by a shared tragedy?

Rehearsing the truths in community helped us see our reality all the more clearly. We were able to verbalize what had become obvious to us: Pat focused more on enjoying Zach as he was in the present moment and most times didn't want to hear me talk about the things that made me sad. I didn't want to bear my sadness alone and wondered whether Pat was in denial, not seeing things as they really were.

Not only did our perspectives often conflict, but we experienced Zach so differently. Pat continued to do with Zach what he had always done on weekends—take him to a game or watch one on TV, do the family shopping, or just take a nap together.

When I tried to do what I used to do with Zach—talk, pray, read the Bible, and sing worship songs with him—our time together usually ended in frustration and emotional fatigue.

We spilled it all before the small group of caring fellow-sufferers.

Then we explained how counseling was helping us deal with our differences. The phrase I remember most from the sessions with our counselor was, "Be gentle with each other." We knew marriages rarely survive tragedies like ours, and we did not want to lose each other. Our conference small group affirmed the work we were doing in counseling to strengthen our marriage.

The loss was real, genuine, deep, perpetual. And yet our son was still alive. Talking about the dynamics of our circumstances and our relationship felt like drawing a full breath after years of shallow breathing. The tasks of maneuvering schedules and family routines, the budget, mealtimes—everything to accommodate Zach's needs—weren't coming to an end. But we'd built part of a framework for survival.

The conference—and in particular the small group—gave us a safe space where we could be honest with our feelings and have them validated by a group of people who understood deep loss.

During a plenary session at the conference, the speaker invited us to surrender everything to God. Everything.

After several moments of reflecting on and praying about what I was still holding on to, I leaned toward Pat and tearfully asked, "What's coming to your mind?"

"What's coming to yours?"

I choked out, "Zach's full recovery."

Pat added, "In this lifetime," his voice thick with emotion.

"Yes, in this lifetime."

We vowed to continue to do all we could to help Zach have a chance at the strongest recovery possible. But we acknowledged, right then before God, that Zach was His child and Zach's future was and is in His hands to do with as He pleases. For His glory.

My journal entries during the month of my fiftieth birthday show that I called that February the "Month of Tears." Thanks to the conference, some of them were drops of healing rather than heartache.

∞

A few months later, I woke with a fervent determination to go to the field where Zach had been injured, to stand in the place where everything changed.

It wasn't a new idea. After Zach's injury, I had often mentioned my longing to Pat.

"I'm not ready to do that," he told me.

I'd tucked that desire away as I focused on the details of Zach's recovery and caring for our jobs, marriage, and family.

This day, a month after the second anniversary of Zach's

injury, I scheduled a personal retreat to reflect and seek silence and solitude with God. I had Pat's blessing, but not his presence.

After spending the morning reading Scripture and praying, I was anxious to get to the field of that fateful scrimmage at a suburban high school twenty miles from our home. I wanted to retrace Zach's steps that day, pray where the hit happened, find some kind of closure by saying good-bye to Zach as he used to be, and listen for what God had to say to my surrendered heart.

I had never been to the school before. With each mile that passed, my heart beat faster. As I rounded the corner of the school and headed down the long driveway that led to the field, I began to unravel.

A soccer match was in full swing when I pulled into a parking spot beside the field. I couldn't turn back. Since I was dressed in my running clothes, I ran laps around the track to pass the time. The soccer match finally wound down, and cars started to pull out.

Good. I'll finally be alone. I have to be alone.

And then a caravan of cars appeared. Two more soccer teams and their fans arrived for a game. My heart sank as I retreated to the car.

I sat there an hour and a half and read, hearing the muted sounds of whistles and cheers. Finally, the second match ended, and the last car drove away.

With a blanket under my arm, I got out of the car. The sun was setting. Dusk settled over me.

At last, I stood alone on the field. I dropped my blanket in a heap on the 36-yard line and took in a panoramic view—the stands, the team benches, the goalposts, the end zones, the white stripes, the hash marks, and the numbers painted on the grass.

Finally, mimicking the team's video footage Pat and I had watched many times—a video that showed nothing conclusive, nothing we could point to that said, "There! That's the moment it happened"—I retraced Zach's path on the field, from his interception to his touchdown in the series before the play in which he was injured. I remembered what his teammates told me about jumping all over Zach in the end zone after he'd scored, how they kept congratulating him and celebrating the great play even after they returned to the sidelines. What a moment that must have been for Zach.

I rewound the mental footage once more and ran through the play again, this time out of breath at the end, sensing the joy he must have experienced scoring his first varsity touchdown.

Then I paused. After who knows how many minutes, I ran, only once, the play on which Zach was injured. Slowly and deliberately I traced the last steps of Zach's football career and collapsed where he and three teammates tackled the ball carrier—the 35-yard line. He fell forward to the 36-yard line. There I spread my blanket.

I lay flat on my back and looked at the expanse of the darkening sky. It was silent except for a few birds singing.

After a long stretch of quiet, I thanked God for all the people He'd used to keep Zach alive that night: coaches, athletic trainers, EMTs, helicopter pilots, nurses, doctors, and surgeons. After a few minutes of spoken prayer, I returned to silence. God was there in the stillness.

It was difficult to leave. Leaving meant moving on.

∞

A month later I found myself moving on in an unexpected way—riding the escalator to the second floor of the Boston Sheraton to speak to the community about Zach's injury and its effect on our family.

In 2010, the NFL—under pressure regarding football-related head injuries—conducted forums called "NFL Community Huddle: Taking a Goal Line Stand for Your Mind and Body" in conjunction with the Morehouse School of Medicine in major US cities. As the mother of a young man directly affected, I was invited to give our family's perspective on the issue. Pat was out of town.

The room was full of former NFL players, community members, and organizers. I met the speakers: a former surgeon general, a medical journalist and moderator, a former Buffalo Bills player, a woman whose husband suffered from early onset dementia as a result of playing pro football, a former Detroit Lions quarterback, and a college athlete who walked away from the game during his first year after suffering multiple concussions.

Each speaker was powerful; I especially appreciated hearing from the players and spouses who continue to suffer from physical, intellectual, emotional, and relational consequences of head injuries. But one sentence seared my heart, spoken to me during a question-and-answer period.

A leading concussion expert said, "Your son may have had second impact syndrome."

I responded, "Yes, he *may* have."

His statement triggered the return of questions that

had haunted me at night during the third month of Zach's injury when I first learned about second impact syndrome—catastrophic brain swelling or bleeding resulting from a *second* concussion before the symptoms of an earlier one have subsided.

After the expert's pronouncement at the NFL event, guilt returned. *Had we missed something the week before when Zach mentioned a headache?* In the past, my only relief from the guilt was to pray and review what I knew to be true about God, about me, and about our situation with Zach. This time, in addition to praying and reviewing truth as I had in the past, I talked about it with our counselor. When Zach was injured in 2008, concussions were not part of our national conversation, and neither was second impact syndrome.

The counselor reminded me—not for the first time—that we couldn't know what we didn't know. We weren't to blame, but I still had to ask God for help when intrusive and condemning thoughts intermittently invaded my mind.

Pat recalled another conversation with the traumatic brain injury doctor at the rehab hospital. To ensure we knew that there was not complete consensus on the topic, he gave us a research paper that refuted the existence of second impact syndrome.

We would never know for certain.

I did know one thing for sure: It was time to let go of guilt for good.

13

Pat

On January 1, 2012, I checked myself into a hotel room in Albany, New York. More than three years had passed since Zach's—and our family's—hard hit. It was obvious he wasn't going to have a strong recovery. I had begun the long, muddy army-crawl toward accepting the fact that "getting over it" was something I would never do, but "moving on" was something I would have to embrace.

The counselor Tammy and I had been seeing was trying to help us make the transition, in his words, "from taking heroic measures to give Zach the greatest chance for a full recovery, to having a long-haul view that involves accepting the likelihood that Zach is going to live life—possibly twenty or more years beyond your lifetimes—with significant physical and mental disabilities."

It required us to start thinking and planning for how to invest in his long-term care and well-being, as well as the long-term care and well-being of our other three children and ourselves. Our expectations for the future had been wrecked. It was time to let go of those expectations and adjust to a new, inescapable reality.

Much like the first time I drove a car with manual transmission, a lot of gear-grinding accompanied this shift in our life's focus and pace. Together, we wrestled with expectations we never knew we had about our vocational ambitions, our lifestyle, our family, and our marriage. Our marriage.

From the moment a crisis hits, every marriage becomes an at-risk marriage. We couldn't allow ours to suffer from lack of attention, from circumstantial neglect.

We'd made progress through counseling and our decision to let go of our expectation that Zach would have a full recovery in this lifetime. It stood as a critical milestone in our journey as a couple.

But moving on involved acknowledging new losses related to Zach's injury that had yet to be grieved. We had lost a lot of time with our other kids during the previous three-plus years. Chelsea was only one semester away from college graduation. Nate was looking at college options. Soren navigated middle school. And still, family life revolved around or at least was influenced by Zach's needs, demands, and even his exuberant, screeching voice.

And I was beginning to face up to losses related to my professional life.

Progress toward certain career goals had slowed to a crawl. This reignited old insecurities about my self-worth. Had I become overzealous in my obligations toward Zach and in so doing missed opportunities and neglected my professional responsibilities? As much as I loved him, was I resigned to serve as caregiver now? Not world changer, or scholar, or leader of a vibrant and growing ministry? Could I be content caring for one young man, my son, when my driving passion had always been to influence a broader sphere of humanity? Were those dreams over? Shelved?

Had I exchanged those pursuits or let them fade because of my focus on Zach? Yes, I had. I wanted Zach home as much as possible. I loved taking him with me whenever I traveled around New England to watch Nate row in a regatta or Soren play Amateur Athletic Union (AAU) basketball. When Tammy had other commitments, it gave me time to connect just with Zach. Driving in silence next to him or having him lay his head on my shoulder as we traveled down the road never got old for me.

For Tammy, the activities she most loved sharing with Zach—talking, singing, and praying aloud together—were not just harder; they were not possible.

I responded by offering to take more responsibility for Zach when he was home. But it didn't solve the problem. It made it worse. Like poking at a bruise, I unknowingly kept smashing the pain of Tammy's greatest loss in her face. And pushing my life and career goals further from my reach.

At the same time, I began to brood over Tammy not experiencing Zach the way I did or not wanting to help out more, despite what I said about taking primary responsibility for him.

Watching me try to do so much by myself heaped more feelings of guilt onto Tammy, I later discovered. She grew increasingly concerned about the way our new lifestyle was taking more and more out of me, robbing us of quality time as a couple, and effectively removing all spontaneity. Nothing could be done without careful preplanning and contingency plan upon contingency plan.

The enormous amounts of energy and time required to plan and pull off each weekend prevented us from spending intentional uninterrupted time with our other kids, nurturing our relationships with friends, and catching up on personal responsibilities. In my attempts to be a great dad to Zach, I was neglecting to love, pursue, and care for the rest of my family.

Over the course of our many counseling sessions and living out what we had learned through them, it had become increasingly clear to Tammy and me that we had been drawn into some of the most painful and least understood parts of life and faith.

I craved the kind of focus I lived with in previous seasons of life but would likely never have again. I had driven into a fog. Progress in every dimension of living slowed to a crawl.

Dragging all this emotional and relational baggage behind me, I stepped into the lobby of a hotel in New York, hoping that four days away from Boston and away from my family would help clear the fog. I wasn't checking into the hotel for a personal retreat; I was there for a conference with hundreds of college students and ministry colleagues. But for the first time in two decades, I was coming to this annual event alone, without my family. Tammy had stayed home to take care of Zach, Nate, and Soren.

After getting my room key, I slowly wheeled my suitcase down the hallway, quietly opened the door, and stepped into the dark room. With a heavy sigh, I threw my bag onto the bed.

Well, at least I don't have to fight someone over the remote.

The last thing I would prescribe for a person in my state of mind at that moment would be to turn on a TV. But I didn't heed my own advice.

I flipped through channels until I found ESPN *SportsCenter*. The commentators were talking about that year's NFL sensation—the Denver Broncos quarterback Tim Tebow. I'd grown up a Broncos fan and was thrilled when the team experienced a complete midyear turnaround under Tebow's leadership. I was fascinated by the young athlete's character and the genuineness with which he spoke about his personal relationship with Jesus Christ.

A few days earlier, I had been interviewed by a *Boston Globe* reporter looking for a sound bite from a Christian authority at Harvard addressing the public nature of Tebow's personal faith. I had Tebow on my mind and was eager to catch up on all the news relating to him and the Broncos.

Before I could finish unpacking my suitcase, ESPN *SportsCenter* finished one feature story on Tebow, touched on a couple of other stories in the sports world, and was already back to Tebow. Every fourth or fifth story featured Tebow. If they were not talking about his controversial public displays of faith, they were replaying the highlights of his noteworthy year.

I'd told the *Globe* reporter that what I found most impressive about this sensational season was not the six fourth-quarter come-from-behind victories he orchestrated after taking over the team partway through the season, but the way Tim provided a window into the qualities of character that made a team so strong. He consistently ducked reporters' attempts to make it all about him—the individual. Instead, he continually redirected the focus onto his teammates, the powerful Broncos' defense, their clutch kicker, their unselfish and hardworking receivers, their coaches, and his God-directed gratitude.

Football had been a hot topic in our family for three years. But despite how our son's traumatic brain injury had changed his life and ours, in my mind at least, football hadn't lost its appeal—for the very reasons touched on by Tim Tebow.

Something stirred in me. I couldn't define it yet. Among all the dichotomies in our lives, was it possible football was both builder and destroyer? And that this star athlete had figured out something I hadn't?

Later that night, I called Marty. I hoped he might help lift the fog I was in. I updated him on the many blows against our marriage and family, as well as concerns I had about failures in my professional life and how I felt my impact and influence on others had dissipated since Zach's brain injury. Our conversation was reminiscent of the one I'd had with him over that Greek omelet years earlier. He let me talk until I had nothing more to say, then ended our time with another speculation.

"If I had to guess, I would predict that what has happened to Zach will not only positively influence the impact of your life, but it will positively impact the extent of your ministry. But I don't think you are going to have to seek that or go out and try to make it happen. I think God is just going to bring it to you."

∞

When I arrived home a few days later, I watched the Broncos shock the football world by knocking off the Pittsburgh Steelers in yet another come-from-behind, overtime victory. The Broncos' next playoff game against the New England Patriots would be played in Boston on Saturday.

The following day, while Tammy and I rushed around the house to get our bags packed for a short trip to Arizona to see my dad, who was battling cancer, my phone buzzed. The caller was the director of W15H—the Tebow Foundation's wish-granting program. Having learned about Zach's tragic injury and inspiring efforts at recovery, the foundation invited Zach to meet with Tim on the field at Gillette Stadium right before the game. The director warned that, in the wake of recent press, a media blitz would likely follow the announcement that Zach had been chosen to be the next W15H recipient.

Tammy and I immediately called Zach at his school.

"Zach, you won't believe what just happened." I didn't have the time or the heart to prolong the suspense. "How would you like to meet Tim Tebow this weekend?"

"Huhhh?"

"Tim Tebow's foundation called and asked if you'd like to meet him at Gillette Stadium at the playoff game on Saturday."

Following a dramatic but predictable—for Zach— pause, we and everyone within earshot heard a very loud "Yeaaaaahhhhhhhh!"

Before we could even board our plane to Arizona, the media blitz began. We had our first interview with the *Boston Herald* as we stood in line at the airport gate. The five-hour flight to Phoenix—without cell reception or internet connection—proved to be the only calm we experienced for the next five days.

On the plane, we tuned into ESPN on the individual TV screens in front of our seats. Tim continued to be the topic of every fourth or fifth feature, which allowed Tammy to catch up with the Tebow-mania that was spreading across the country.

Before we awoke the next morning, I had already missed two calls from an eager reporter for *USA Today*. Shortly after I called him back, Tammy and I were on speakerphone, answering the reporter's questions. The next day, the paper's front page included a feature on Zach. Later that week, HLN (owned by CNN) also interviewed Zach and Tammy live.

Throughout that week, we were contacted by a number of other local and national print and broadcast media. In every interview, Zach won over each reporter, cameraman, and lighting person who came within hugging distance. The story went viral. One Harvard Business School student told us he'd watched the live HLN interview from a hotel room in India.

The much-anticipated meeting between Tim and Zach was set for 7:30 Saturday night. We flew Chelsea home from college and, with Zach, Nate, and Soren, picked her up on the way to the stadium. The director of the Tebow Foundation escorted us onto the field, where we watched the players warm up. Tim's parents, siblings, and several friends trickled in. They made Zach and our whole family feel like part of theirs. Zach could barely—could *not*—contain his excitement and took everything in with his typical loud exuberance.

Demaryius Thomas, who had made the 80-yard game-winning catch for Denver the previous week, came over to meet Zach. Our son landed a couple of solid hugs on number 88 before letting him go.

A few minutes later, Tim trotted toward us. With a look of pure joy on his face, Zach lunged onto the field and gave him a bear hug. Tim reciprocated and handed Zach a football, lingering a few minutes longer, as if he hadn't a care in the world. Then he introduced himself to each member of our family.

Tim hugged and high-fived Zach once more. "I'll see you after the game, all right?"

Zach smiled and nodded.

Tim left for the locker room. We settled in for what we hoped would be another great chapter in the Broncos' miraculous season.

But it was not to be. The Patriots jumped out to an early lead and never looked back.

The Broncos lost 45–10. Tim was sacked five times and would find out the next day that he had suffered a fractured collarbone and rib.

As the final minutes ticked off the clock, we began to gather our things to leave. The foundation director appeared out of nowhere and said, "Come with me. Tim wants to spend more time with Zach."

Tammy and our other kids were left at the security point when the director led Zach and me to a restricted area reserved for coaches, players, and the press. We stopped outside a room where Tim was finishing a press conference, answering a final question about whether he believed he had proven to himself, the organization, and his critics that he could play quarterback at this level.

Without hesitation, Tim replied that this wasn't the focus of his attention. He was disappointed that they didn't win and gave credit to the skill of the opposing team.

"It still was a good day," Tebow said, "because before the game I got to spend time with Zach McLeod and make him smile. Overall, when you get to do that it's still a positive day and a good day. Sometimes it's just hard to see, but it depends what lens you're looking through. I choose to look through those lenses, and I got to make a kid's day and anytime you do that it's more important than winning a game, so I'm proud of that."

With that, Tim stepped away from the mic. The moment he exited the stage, Zach spotted Tim and took off running to give him another hug. Showing no sign of a fractured rib and collarbone, Tim reciprocated.

When we reunited with the rest of our families, Chelsea told Tim, "Speaking comes hard for Zach, so on the way down here, we asked Zach to type what he wanted to say to you. Would it be okay if we read what he typed?"

"Absolutely," Tim replied.

"I should warn you," Chelsea added, "that due to the nature of Zach's injury, he relies on his right brain, which is definitely the more creative hemisphere. As a result, Zach tends to add a few original flourishes to words whenever he types a message."

Tim smiled at Zach, who shook his head and gave his classic *my bad* face as he patted his left hand against his chest—his own version of sign language for "I'm sorry."

Chelsea turned on the iPad and read Zach's note.

Um, hey there, broski, would you like to pray with me sometime? No pressure or anything like that. Stay strong there berudder bearski [Zach's word for big brother]. From your bruther in Christ, Zach McLeod.

Without hesitation, Tim pulled Zach into a huddle of two. Closing their eyes and bowing their heads, the two *broskies* talked to their heavenly Father.

Tammy

On the Monday after the game, we stepped through the doors of the HLN/CNN studio. They had asked for a follow-up interview, this time with all three of us. Pat, Zach, and I were led through a large room filled with television monitors, as well as HLN/CNN producers and editors at their desks. We were shown to a small room with three chairs, several lights, and one large camera. The sound technician hooked up our mics, and then we were on the air, responding to questions.

Zach once again stole the show with his exuberant smiles and high energy. But because of his limited speaking ability, the anchor looked to us to fill in the blanks of Zach's interaction with Tim. I told the interviewer about the initial meeting and the joy of being introduced not just to Tim, but to the entire Tebow family.

Pat shared some of the similarities and differences between Zach's and Tim's high-drama football stories. Tim's football career, from all reports, was gaining momentum. Zach's was over. Tim's football story was as dramatically triumphant as Zach's was tragic. But a shared belief in a larger story bonded their hearts together. It provided them both with a sense of meaning, purpose, and joy that sustained and stabilized their lives.

So much fanfare. Zach had become an overnight celebrity. But two elements of the experience colored it for me. Like it or not, we were being plunged deeper and deeper into a national conversation about the collision between football and brain injury. And our son was being recognized not for what he *could* do, but for what he couldn't.

Pat

A half hour after the interview, Tammy and I stepped out of the doors of the television studio with Zach. It had been a little over two weeks since I had checked myself into that lonely hotel room with all my emotional baggage in tow, lost in a fog of confusion—knowing I would never get over it but needed to get on with it.

I couldn't have imagined the unlikely journey God would take us on. My career crisis wasn't over. But Tim and Zach provided the lens I had been searching for to bring career and life priorities back into focus.

With greater clarity, I caught a vision of the larger story that provided meaning, inspiration, consolation, and hope to the smaller stories of our lives. I could better see how the Author of that larger story uses whatever happens to us to make an impact in and through us. The possibility of influencing "the broader sphere" wasn't over for me because I'd needed to and chosen to focus so much attention on Zach. But my goals as well as my understanding of that influence were changing.

As Marty predicted, the force of that impact would not come from chasing local, national, or international television broadcasts, nabbing front-page headlines, or even winning championship games. Rather, as Tim and Zach had shown me, it would come through simple microevents of kindness, connection, and communion with God and others.

14

Tammy

A house as old as ours is in a perpetual state of needing repairs. More than a hundred years of residents opening and closing cupboard doors, pounding up and down the stairs, scuffing across the hardwood floors, and raising and lowering the windows in concert with Boston's alternating heat and cold takes its toll.

Four years after Zach's injury, I joined the October House Work Day event organized by the manager of the property.

Somehow I tweaked a muscle in my neck while moving heavy cupboards. It was a two-person job. I should have known better.

I iced it that night, but by morning I knew *tweak* wasn't the right word to use. As much as I abhorred working a doctor's appointment into an already busy schedule, there was no avoiding it.

Just as there was no avoiding the unexpected results of the neck scan. I had thyroid cancer.

Pat

I can't explain the swirl of emotions when Tammy told me the test results.

"If you're going to get cancer," the doctors had told her, "this is the one to get."

Small comfort. It was still cancer.

"Treatable," they'd said.

Still cancer.

Still my wife. Still a woman who'd had to be strong for all of us through the unthinkable we'd been enduring. Nate broke down when we told him. Shock masked Soren's face. Chelsea's voice on the phone was supportive but held the same sense of disbelief.

Diagnosed in October, Tammy shuffled between Zach's doctor's appointments and her own through November. We heard the word *surgery* and spent more time wondering how we'd work it into our work/family/Zach schedules than we did wondering about the outcome.

But I did wonder. Was the recurring emotional numbness protective or delusion? We had to get through the surgery scheduled for January so we could move on. To the next thing. There was always a next thing.

The medical staff spoke in reassuring tones that seemed to do little more than add to the noise.

It would be an interesting Christmas, waiting for January.

∞

On a Friday night that December, I was working at my desk in the study of our second-floor apartment. I wanted to get as much done as possible before Zach arrived home for the weekend. My concentration was broken by a loud, unsettling noise, followed by a house-shaking *thud. What in the world was that?*

Chelsea had graduated from college and no longer lived at home. Nate was studying for finals. Soren was at a basketball tournament. And Tammy had gone to pick up Zach.

The eerie silence that followed the deafening *thud* heightened my concern. What could have caused the entire house to shake? I pulled open the back door to our apartment just as one of our housemates raced toward me up the ancient winding steps.

"Zach fell over the banister and is lying on the floor, unconscious!" he panted.

How was that possible? In three or four strides, I stumbled down the thirteen steep steps and slid onto the floor where Zach was lying on his side. Motionless.

"Zach? Zach?"

No response. He wasn't breathing.

Kiley, another of our housemates, called for an ambulance.

"Zach, breathe! Breathe, Zach!" My pleas couldn't rouse him.

But then his eyes opened, and he struggled to lift his head, as if trying to take a breath. His eyes rolled back, eyelids closed, and his head fell against the hard floor.

"Zach! Zach! Breathe! Breathe, Zach!" I shouted, more forcefully each time. I tried to adjust his position. There was blood in his mouth, but no blood on the floor, no lump on his head. His backpack was still strapped to his back.

"Should I get Tammy?" Kiley asked.

The confusion of the scene deepened. I thought Tammy had gone to get Zach at the school.

"I don't want her to see him like this." *I don't want her to watch her son die.*

Where is the ambulance?

"Zach, breathe!"

An eternity passed in those few minutes. *Get Tammy? What did Kiley mean? How did Zach get here? Who was with him? Why was he alone? Why was he coming up the spiral staircase we never let him use?* All these questions flooded my mind in an instant.

When at last I heard the first faint sounds of one siren and then another, a rush of relief pulsed through my body. Help was on its way. Within seconds, EMTs and firemen surrounded Zach. He took a breath. I stepped back and began answering the questions I could and listening to our housemates answer those I couldn't.

I had no idea that Tammy was home until she joined me at Zach's side. She had seen the lights of the ambulance from her bedroom on the second floor. That's the first she knew that Zach's life once again hung over a precipice. Neither of us could imagine what had happened. We knew only one thing—our son was lying lifeless on the tile floor at the base of the stairs.

As the EMTs loaded Zach onto a stretcher, I asked if we could accompany him. I was told that only one of us would be allowed to ride in the ambulance with our son. While Tammy consoled the shaken-up residents, I ran upstairs to grab what I needed, slapping the door as hard as I could, and yelled out in anguish as I ran through the house. *How could this have happened?* A few minutes later, I followed two firemen and two EMTs as they wheeled Zach out the front door. Tammy said she would notify the kids and get to the hospital—Massachusetts General this time—as soon as possible.

When we finally burst through the emergency doors of Mass General, a team of eight medical personnel stood at attention, awaiting our arrival. Like a well-oiled machine, they went to work on Zach. Within minutes, they stabilized his breathing, took X-rays, and determined that though he had fractured a vertebra and a shoulder blade, there appeared to be no spinal-cord injury. Zach regained consciousness and began responding to commands.

For a few moments, I entertained the possibility that his brain had emerged from the fall unscathed, and despite the heart-wrenching drama, this was not going to be a big deal. Those hopes were dashed when a CT scan revealed a subdural hematoma almost identical to his previous brain injury.

Zach needed yet another emergency brain surgery.

∞

While we waited for the surgery's conclusion, Tammy and I combined our stories plus what Tammy had learned from the first-floor residents. We pieced together what had happened.

Zach had been dropped off at the house by the new public transportation service that had recently taken over the job of bringing him to us from the May Center School each weekend.

The school had recommended we start using the service, since we'd soon be using it routinely.

Normally the school's van brought him directly to our weekly meeting in downtown Boston. Without my knowing it, Tammy had arranged for them to bring him to our house that night, since there was no meeting because of college Christmas break. She had not gone to the school to pick him up. She had never left the house.

Tammy had been in her office upstairs. She'd been down the hallway from my study, far enough away not to have heard and felt the thud.

Instead of bringing Zach to the entrance that led directly to our apartment, the new transportation service had brought him to the main door of the house. We traditionally briefed our fellow housemates at the beginning of the school year about basic safety issues relating to Zach. They knew he was never allowed to go up *any* steps unattended. But the one resident who happened to answer the door that night had moved into the house midsemester and had not gotten the briefing. She was not to blame.

When the resident opened the door, Zach enthusiastically hugged her. This was proof enough to the driver that his job was finished. He turned Zach over to her rather than to us.

Not knowing that she was supposed to get us or that Zach was only allowed on the main stairway to our second-floor apartment, the one with special safety handrails for him, the young woman stepped back, returning to what she was doing.

Zach had bolted up the ancient winding stairs to our back-door entrance. In his eagerness to see us, Zach tried to take two stairs in one step at the top of the staircase, the young woman who let him in said. Apparently, because of the permanent weakness in his right leg and the weight of his heavy pack, he lost his balance and started falling backward. He tried grabbing the railing but failed because the banister was wrapped with Christmas garlands.

The perfect storm of circumstances came together. Zach stumbled, flipped over the railing, and fell twelve feet, landing on his upper back and side.

And now his fragile brain was once more the center of a surgeon's attention.

Tammy

Zach's fall over the banister was the kind of thing for which the term *freak accident* was coined. Everything that could have gone right didn't. Everything that could go wrong did.

I couldn't get the sound of the sirens out of my head. Even as I'd called the other kids and rushed to pull together what I'd need at the hospital, deep in my brain I still heard the screams of the sirens pulling away from our house. Just when we thought we had begun a peaceful adjustment to living with Zach's situation, our whole world came crashing down again.

Within the hour, Zach was wheeled into surgery. And just like last time, our team of friends immediately began taking care of us. Messages went out over the internet and by phone. People poured into the waiting room as we all tried to absorb the news. After more than four arduous years of hospitalization and rehabilitation, Zach was back in a sterile operating room with a team of surgeons cauterizing blood vessels and extracting blood from his brain cavity. I couldn't wrap my mind around it.

We quickly stepped into our own all-too-familiar roles, roles we now navigated with a sense of partnership. When surgery was over, Pat spent the night at the hospital with Zach. I returned home to normalize things as much as possible for Nate and Soren and try to get some sleep so I could relieve Pat in the morning. All too familiar.

Zach's condition continued to improve over the next two days. On the fourth day, though, the brain surgeon expressed concern about swelling under the skin around the wound. Earlier that morning, the doctor had drained half a cup of fluid from the area. By the end of the day, that fluid had replaced itself, suggesting it was cerebrospinal brain fluid. Zach had become hydrocephalic; the tissue around his brain was not absorbing spinal fluid as fast as his brain was producing it.

By the next day, Zach's wound had become so swollen that brownish-yellow fluid began leaking out of the stitched holes and onto his pillow. Zach needed a permanent shunt implanted surgically to drain the liquid. His brain surgeon explained that if they put the shunt on the outside of the skullcap, they would run the risk of infection or the shunt could become clogged. But if they put it on the inside of the skullcap, they would run the risk of injuring the healthiest portion of Zach's brain and potentially altering his personality.

Impossible options. Pat and I agreed, though, that we would rather risk infection than risk altering Zach's personality. We asked the surgeon to insert the shunt on the outside of his skullcap.

The fear that this procedure would fail loomed over us as the medical staff prepped our son for yet another surgery. My own pending thyroid surgery rarely crossed my mind. Zach was lying in a gloomy, sterile hospital bed with a bulging C-shaped incision on his freshly shaven head—again—with cerebrospinal fluid still seeping from his head onto the pillowcase. He pulled us toward him for hugs, everything in slow motion.

The team released the brake on Zach's bed and wheeled our son away. It was all I could do to resist plastering the ceiling with the words, "How much more, Lord? How much more can any of us take?"

Pat

The prognosis was not good. Zach's brain had taken another beating—literally. Somehow, his right brain had been spared major injury again. As a result, many characteristics that had always made Zach so life-giving to me remained intact—his creativity, sense of humor, emotional intelligence, empathy, and ability to take nonverbal cues. But if this procedure failed, he ran the risk of losing these qualities as well. The Zach we knew and loved would be lost.

Looking at Zach's smiling face against the backdrop of his damp pillow did me in. I gave up the battle of holding back tears and focused instead on keeping myself from sobbing. When I lost that battle, I excused myself in hopes of finding a place where I could wail. As I searched, I felt a vibration in my pocket. Marty was calling. I found a chair in the corridor of the pre-op room, put my head down and said, "Marty."

Between deep gasps, I tried to spit out what was happening. He listened patiently—as he always did. I composed myself enough to finally eke out, "I love him so much."

Marty understood what was happening in the silence that followed.

I wanted to say how thankful I was to experience a father-son bond so strong that I would feel the intensity of emotion coursing through my body at that moment, but I just couldn't do it.

Marty waited.

"I guess this is what love feels like," I finally said.

More silence.

Eventually I explained, "If this procedure doesn't work . . ." My mouth resisted forming the rest of the words, but my soul shoved them out. "I'm afraid of losing him."

In some ways, I suppose I was getting a taste of the sense of loss that Tammy had been living with for more than four years.

∞

Another week passed. Zach battled pneumonia and a bladder infection. Although those eventually cleared, an accompanying fever that occasionally spiked to 103 degrees continued to assault him and worry doctors. After ruling out other causes, the medical staff suspected the culprit responsible for the infection and corresponding fever was the artificial shunt they had placed in Zach's head.

It appeared their attempt to avoid a more invasive surgery had not succeeded. With no options left, the shunt would have to be removed and a new one inserted directly into the brain cavity, risking injury to the right side of Zach's brain and potentially altering his temperament.

Before risking that surgery, the team needed to determine conclusively that the shunt was the source of the infection. They drew a sample of Zach's spinal fluid from his back and cultured it. We began the two-day waiting game to see if bacteria grew in the culture.

Tammy and I returned home without our son, grateful that the holiday break had given us time off work just when we needed it. We used those days to reconnect with Nate, Soren, and Chelsea, who were rocked by another blow to their brother's prognosis on top of their concern for their mother's thyroid surgery.

We updated a host of caring friends. Sobered by the continual flow of hard hits and the risk Zach faced—pending the outcome of the spinal fluid culture—words came hard. Tammy and I functioned by rote, but conscious of each other's needs and aware that Tammy's upcoming surgery—unavoidable—would happen while Zach was still at Mass General.

Between his brain and shunt surgeries, the broken vertebra and scapula, the pneumonia and urinary infections, Zach had been almost completely confined to a bed and had spent the major portion of every day sleeping. He wore an upper body cast when he sat upright, but it could be removed when he was lying down.

About an hour after we left the hospital one evening, Zach's nurse went into his room to get him settled for the night. When she opened the door, she was horrified at the sight of Zach's empty bed. Where had he gone? His upper body cast lay beside the bed. His monitors and IV tree were on the other side of the bed. But Zach was gone.

Panicked, the nurse was terrified at the thought that her brain trauma patient with a broken back, who had hardly moved in two weeks, may have tried to climb over the bed railings and fallen. She bolted to the other side of the room. There he was, on the floor. But he was not on his back or on his side, or unconscious, or even struggling. She found him kneeling peacefully, hands clasped, elbows on the floor, head bowed, praying, with IVs and monitors still attached.

Somehow Zach had pulled off his prayer escape.

He was completely baffled by all the fuss that went into getting him back in bed and making sure he was okay. He was—according to the nurse who informed us of his escapade the next morning—a little miffed that the nurses had interrupted a very satisfying prayer time.

"And as you see," she added, "we have taken appropriate measures to ensure it won't happen again."

From the doorway where we stood talking, I could see Zach working harder than Houdini to escape from the security belt now strapped around his waist. Clearly, Zach was not happy about this new arrangement and what it would mean for his preferred posture when conversing with his heavenly Father.

The lab results showed no signs of infection in Zach's spinal fluid. Doctors grew more hopeful that the shunt was working again and the dreaded surgery unnecessary. Zach's condition continued to improve.

And all the while my wife was preparing for cancer surgery.

Tammy

I woke from the thyroidectomy groggy, but grateful. One more thing out of the way. My main concern before the thyroid surgery had been that the surgeon might nick my vocal cords. That had happened to my friend. She has a hard time speaking loudly anymore. Would I sing again?

Once the operation was over, the surgeon said all had gone well, that I should have no trouble speaking or singing. After all the hard news we'd endured, his assessment was a welcome relief.

Pat

The poignancy of shuttling between my son's hospital and my wife's—Massachusetts Eye and Ear Infirmary—buildings nearly side by side, added to the surreal atmosphere.

Seeing Tammy right after her surgery jolted me. For the first time in my life, my strong and beautiful lover and partner looked so vulnerable. I realized that I had too often taken for granted the remarkable resilience of the woman I love.

Those feelings, though powerful, were fleeting. By the time I arrived at the hospital the next morning, Tammy had turned her room into an office and was fast at work with her computer, files, and thank-you notes all over the tray table.

Three months earlier, cancer had inserted its rude self into our lives. Now it was gone. Both Tammy and Zach had been given permission to keep living.

Zach was ready to be transferred to his old home at Spaulding Rehab Hospital. Surprising us all, considering what he'd gone through, he made daily gains. Small, but notable. Within five weeks, he was ready to go back to the May Center School.

Tammy rebounded with a tenacity that left me in awe. She stepped back into serving, loving, and giving as if she'd had to do no more than take a long weekend before resuming life without the nagging gnat of cancer. A remarkable woman.

Her voice had dropped a few decibels and had a huskier quality to it. But she hadn't been taken from me.

15

Pat

It wasn't our imagination that told us Zach had not rebounded well from his fall. Several months into his recovery, we gathered for a progress report from Zach's therapists, teachers, social workers, and residential staff. As each person around the conference table gave an update on Zach's status since returning to the May Center School, a collective sadness began to settle over us.

Zach's deficits since the fall over the stair rail were more acute than before. He had not yet returned to baseline in any area. Progress had either slowed or stopped on every front. A heaviness hovered over the room as each report followed the same chorus—balance was worse, speech was worse, use of the right hand was worse, walking was worse, attention was worse, short-term memory was worse.

One brutally honest and discouraging report followed another. Then came an extended pause. With a confused look on her face, Stacey, Zach's physical therapist, interrupted the somber silence. "But one thing I *have* noticed is that Zach seems happier than ever."

A flurry of anecdotes affirming that observation flew back and forth across the table among therapists with mounting enthusiasm over Zach's joyful spirit. Everyone in the room agreed. Zach was somehow, inexplicably, happier than ever.

Despite the setbacks, his exuberant personality remained undamaged. It relieved some of the sting of the overall prognosis. No struggle, it seemed, could erase his joy.

The realization took me back to the night before Zach's fall. Our family had attended our church's "Blue Christmas Service," an event designed to acknowledge and validate the pain and suffering in each of our experiences. At Christmas, grief and pain can easily be obscured, dismissed, or ignored amid the festivities and celebrations surrounding the season. We were grateful for a church that noticed and planned an event to honor how difficult the holidays can be for those in chronic pain; those caregiving for a spouse or other family member nearing life's end; those whose children were missing from the table or in danger; widows and widowers; orphans; those without homes or hope.

In words and music, silence and prayer, the service gave the hurting permission to *admit* their sorrow, the assurance that they were loved, and that their distress was not lost on their church family. Tammy participated in the service using one of her strongest gifts—music. The lyrics Tammy sang shed light now on Stacey's comment at the May Center School about Zach's happiness:

> *There is no disease or no struggle*
> *That can pull you from God, be ye glad*

Tammy

In a string of hard hits, the confirmation that Zach had significantly regressed in every area fought for dominance. The May Center School staff shifted gears and scheduled yet another meeting, this time to lay out their final plan—their final plays. The Center's program was designed to end when a resident turned twenty-two. Zach had one year left at that school. It was time to start thinking long-term.

Our reluctant journey with deep brain trauma had begun when our son was sixteen, almost seventeen. Now at twenty-one, he was about to enter a new era—aging out of the May Center School system.

We could see the physical evidence of Zach's scars. It was gut-wrenching to consider how deeply they had cut into the fabric of our other children's emotional, relational, and spiritual formation. Soren had spent a third of his life coping with his older brother's—with our whole family's—trauma. Chelsea had experienced the entirety of her college years with her parents knee-deep in one phase or another of focus on Zach. Nate's high school years, despite our best intentions, had lacked our fully engaged presence.

But even those concerns had to be tabled for the crisis at

hand. What now? What would the May Center team suggest during that upcoming long-term strategy meeting?

In addition to the anticipated school transition, the rehab doctor who had been with Zach from his first days at Spaulding, a man who had prayed for Zach and tried everything he knew to position our son for a strong recovery, was moving to Washington, DC. He'd been called to develop a new program for those who suffered traumatic brain injury in the military.

Saying good-bye to this lead doctor at Zach's final appointment with him was difficult. He knew our son's situation intimately and shared our faith commitment, but he would no longer be involved in Zach's healing process. Pat was out of town at the time, which made the parting even more stressful for me.

For the follow-up meeting to discuss Zach's transition from the school to something more permanent, Pat was again scheduled to be out of town.

There couldn't have been a worse week for him to be gone. I dreaded sitting through the "What do we do now?" planning session with Pat miles away, and I braced myself for the pronouncement of what Zach's life would be like when he had to leave the place that had offered him the care he needed.

Person by person, the fifteen therapists and teachers presented their reports. Pat listened in and commented by phone. Each staff member rehearsed yet again how Zach had regressed as a result of his fall. I took notes but couldn't emotionally process the implications of what they were saying. Eventually, the updates became so overwhelming that I quit writing.

As a group, the staff recommended it was best to stop Zach's academic studies (basic English, science, history, and math) and focus on helping him transition to life as an adult with a debilitating brain injury. It finally sank in that what these staff members had said earlier would be true of our Zach. He would never return to high school. Never get a college degree. He would not be able to support himself or live alone. I knew it also meant that he would never marry or have children, despite our hopes that they'd been wrong. We'd hung on to the idea that Zach would outperform all brain function expectations and—grueling as the recovery might be—regain much of what he'd lost.

Ending academics, facing the encroaching reality that Zach would be severely disabled *for life*, made my stomach clench.

For the first two years after his initial injury, I had kept a journal for Zach in which I briefly recorded what happened in his life every day. When he was fully healed, I wanted to read back to him what had happened so he could know the full story of what he'd come through. As the third year began, I'd switched to journaling for him every few days, and at the end of the third year, I stopped. Every entry would have said, "No change." I couldn't bear to write those words in ink on paper.

I'd held myself together during the transition meeting. But once inside the car for the trip home, I bawled as if my insides had been ripped out.

∞

I thrive on concrete ideas—dreams fleshed out with a clear strategy. As this new wave of sorrow subsided, I concentrated on pursuing what I envisioned for Zach's long-term home. I dove into a proactive effort toward finding a place for Zach to flourish after his May Center School days concluded.

I pored over books about housing options for people with disabilities and visited many places, gathering ideas. I attended housing conferences and talked with individuals who had developed creative living situations for people with challenges like our son's.

Zach needed a home where he could live out his love for God and others, where he could continue to grow and learn, possibly a Christian community where his friends would come for dinners or on weekends. My dream for him was a base from which he could reach out every day to minister to others— orphans, children with disabilities, patients in rehab hospitals.

We wanted to handpick the house and the full-time staff who would be working with Zach. If the house was close to the Harvard campus, maybe even in our Cambridge area of Boston, the students we served could be involved in Zach's life, and we could be near him.

Like a home buyer who augments a list of "must-haves" with a "wish list," I pictured a place close to our home and church, with a layout that included a room with art supplies so Zach could draw and paint again; a room with a small keyboard, djembe, and guitar so he could make music; and a room with a cardio machine and weights so he could work out.

Despite months of work to create our own living situation for Zach right next to where we live, we were denied our request, which left me completely distraught.

One day, the Department of Developmental Services representative called about an opening she had found for Zach in the Massachusetts Association for the Blind (MAB Community Services), a highly regarded organization that serves the blind and visually impaired, but also assists those with traumatic brain injuries. In all my intense searching, I had never seen the agency mentioned. Hope dared to show its face again.

The red brick house in a beautiful residential suburb of Boston welcomed us with its spacious front lawn. Anticipation punctuated each footstep as we neared the entrance. I so hoped it would be a place in which I could picture Zach happy and well cared for.

As soon as the doors opened to us, I felt hope rising. We were greeted warmly, then shown the newly remodeled room that would be Zach's. A beautiful room with red brick walls, a hardwood floor, and light streaming through three large windows.

This could be it. Zach's new home.

Within minutes, we'd observed each staff member's warmth and kindness as they moved naturally through their tasks, attending to needs, and engaged in making each of the four other residents realize the best life possible.

The list of positives grew, but my heart still ached for what I'd envisioned—Zach near us.

Many of the staff members were people of faith. Zach's agemates and soon-to-be housemates were kind and excited about his coming to live with them.

The MABWorks day program Zach would attend from nine to three every day was a great fit for him. Zach could continue to volunteer for his high school's athletic department, folding towels, hanging jerseys, filling ice bags and water bottles, wiping down equipment, and playing the role of manager for various athletic teams, as he had for the past year.

In addition, he could continue rowing at Community Rowing Inc. and participate in other adaptive sports through AccesSportAmerica. He could even join the YMCA through

MAB to gain access to a pool, which would help his balance issues. His day program included music activities, which would ensure he could continue to play guitar.

Most of the bits and pieces of my dream for Zach had been provided by God, but in a different way than I had imagined. In October of 2013, Zach was moved to MAB housing and enrolled in its programs. Another leg of his journey had begun.

CHAPTER

16

Tammy

In the winter of 2014, I sat hunched and anxious in my reading chair. The bay window in my bedroom framed a cold, blustery day in New England as I clung to the hope that I'd find answers for my perpetually gnawing ache within the pages of yet another book on grief.

Yes, we'd been given exceptional opportunities. We were surviving. We were repairing fissures in relationships and coping. Constantly coping.

But I couldn't give up the search for a way to reconcile the simultaneous loss and presence of our son.

Several hours of reading later, I flipped to the final page of the book and sighed. Another book had failed to speak to the suffering of those whose loved one is still alive but is not the same cognitively or emotionally.

I'd been searching not just for our family's sake, but for others like us who had yet to learn the dance steps to life's song when *alive* doesn't mean what it once did. The parents or spouses of stroke victims; those waiting for the return of a prisoner of war—or for the return of the prisoner's remains; parents of a newborn with severe, life-altering medical issues; those who love a person stripped of cognitive function by dementia or Alzheimer's . . .

I'd devoured dozens of books and articles on grief and had hundreds of conversations with caring friends and colleagues. But it wasn't until I reached out to the librarian who worked at the rehab hospital where Zach had been that I found a clue to what I had been searching for. He remembered Zach and our five months in the hospital. I asked specifically if he had any resources that might help.

The next day I received an email response from him. "I think the concept that describes the kind of loss you are experiencing is 'ambiguous loss.'"

It had a name?

The agony we had been living with, which showed no visible shape but bore tangible weight, had a name. *Ambiguous loss.*

The librarian recommended several sources that address our unique type of grief. I immediately devoured the journal articles he had listed and then ordered a book he suggested: *Ambiguous Loss: Learning to Live with Unresolved Grief* by Pauline Boss.

The moment the book arrived, I once again settled into my reading chair. Boss describes two types of ambiguous loss. One is when the body is absent yet the person is psychologically present in the minds of loved ones. Examples include those missing because of war, natural disasters, kidnapping, or divorce.

The other kind of loss, Boss said, occurs when a person is bodily present but is not the same emotionally or cognitively. Examples of this loss include people affected by Alzheimer's, addiction, mental illness, or debilitating brain injury.

The very people who had been on my mind.

Every word, every sentence, every paragraph resonated with my pain. *Ambiguous Loss* validated my conflicted feelings over our situation: In so many ways, Zach was gone but didn't die. What kind of grief is that? *Ambiguous loss.* Finally, I had a description, a legitimization for our experience.

Our pain had a name. The search wasn't wasted. It had led me to this.

Once I'd finished her first book, I tracked down everything I could find by Pauline Boss. In *Loss, Trauma, and Resilience*, she writes: "Closely attached people who become separated through ambiguous loss suffer a trauma even greater than death."

Someone understood.

Zach and I had been so closely attached, connected through music and deep discussions and praying for and with each other. No wonder his situation felt like a trauma even greater than death.

And more. Grieving people often talk about the importance of closure. I had sensed that in our type of loss, there wasn't and shouldn't be closure. *Couldn't* be closure. Zach was still with us.

Pauline Boss confirmed my belief. To pursue closure was a fruitless and impossible endeavor. Instead, the healing words on the pages told me, we needed to "learn how to hold two opposing ideas in [our] minds at the same time." Having and not having.

Our son was still with us—in body—but he wasn't with us cognitively in the same way he had been before the accident.

In that sense, he was gone.

Ambiguity is in part "the maintaining of two or more logically incompatible beliefs or attitudes at the same time."

My focus landed on this anchoring line that brought a breath of understanding, affirmation: Living with continuous uncertainty and loss, according to Boss, *"is the most stressful loss people can face."*

And the ambiguous nature means the edges are undefined by traditional standards. Perhaps a beginning, an inciting moment, but no clear end. No explainable breadth and depth. Nothing to mark its boundaries.

How do we acknowledge or commemorate occasions of great grief or great joy? A funeral recognizes a death, honors the deceased, and is an important step in the grieving process of loved ones. A wedding marks the start of a marriage and serves as a celebration with family and friends. A graduation ceremony and party help launch a young person into a new season of life.

When a loss is ambiguous, no public ceremony acknowledges the loss and its fallout, or honors the memory of the loved one. It was true for us. People still were unsure how to respond to the endlessness of our unique form of loss. Should they grieve with us or pretend life was fine now that Zach had lived through it all? Would we resent it if they didn't mention the injury, or if they did?

As I continued to consider Boss's words on this subject, my mind swept through the years we had just endured. The shock and life disruption of the accident. The multiple surgeries. The hope Zach would "return" to us as he'd been the day he headed to the football scrimmage. The realization that he would never again be as he had once been.

The grieving and agonizing, and the inability to put into words what we were experiencing in a way that our friends and colleagues would understand, had compounded the pain. My struggle to express it adequately to Pat or our other children, who carried their own versions of ambiguous loss, had taken a toll.

We were desperate to hold on and persevere. In the beginning, I'd hoped to find answers and resolve the problems. I'd relentlessly pursued a way to fix what had happened to Zach, to us. But I learned from Boss that I would need to "temper" my desire for what she called "mastery." Fixing it was an unattainable goal. The goal in ambiguous loss is not to get rid of the ambiguity, but to live well with it and increase tolerance for it.

Live well with ambiguous loss.

I resolved to face my unremitting grief anew, having at last found a path to help me move forward. Pat had come to grips with the need to move beyond his relentless expectation of Zach's full recovery. I now had found validation for grieving over a son who was still alive.

It had taken one phone call from a frantic Nate to spin us off into this hurricane of grief called *ambiguous loss.* It took years to find the words to encapsulate what it meant.

Pat

I'll never forget the day Tammy handed me a research paper she'd been working on for grad school. It wasn't surprising that the topic she'd chosen was grief. What surprised me was that she'd found a name for ours.

It's no wonder that it had seemed impossible to navigate, and that our personalities and ways of relating to Zach made the task of carrying two ends of the burden a study in futility. It no longer seemed a curiosity that two faith-filled people could approach the same trauma with opposing perspectives, or that we could vacillate between hope and loss as often as we inhaled and exhaled. Or that corralling our emotions had made us question our sanity at times. Was our sense that we'd experienced a loss worth grieving legitimate or not? Real or imagined?

Ambiguous loss.

Tammy introduced me to the writing Pauline Boss had done on the subject. We weren't alone in our inability to neatly shelve our loss. It was in a category of its own, shared by many others.

Both of us, along with Zach's siblings, were faced with the daunting challenge of holding two thoughts as real—both *having* Zach and *not having* him the way we once did. All forms of ambiguous loss hold those truths in tension.

As I read Tammy's paper, I began to feel like I was listening to the finale of a Broadway musical—the song that melds all the previous songs into one refrain. Every statement about ambiguous loss resonated with the personal and interpersonal drama of our own family. And the whole concept of ambiguous loss resonated with the creation, fall, and redemption theme of the larger story that had carried me through.

I felt my shoulders relax as I read more, noting what Tammy had marked as meaningful to her. I saw Tammy's pain with fresh perspective. Our marriage challenges hadn't been rooted in her rightness/my wrongness or the other way around. They weren't driven by selfishness or selflessness or sadness. It was the *ambiguity* of the loss.

Finding out its name somehow changed things. In a profound way, for the first time in years, we were reading from the same page.

Tammy

Now what? We had a name for our distress, which had gotten in our way like piles of demolition debris and construction tools in a remodeling project with no completion date. We'd been frustrated because all our attempts to work around it seemed to fall short. Giving a name to our grief didn't remove the debris. It didn't finish the project. The facts of what life now looked like, the mounting costs on every level, and the ripped and stained blueprint of Zach's and our futures remained.

We'd taken comfort in God's presence in our mess. We'd drawn strength from those who'd donned work gloves and hard hats to walk through it with us. But knowing what it was called—ambiguous loss—didn't convert the chaos into what anyone would have presumed was a completed project.

What it *had* done was throw light on the scene so we were less prone to trip over extension cords or step on rusty nails. It improved visibility in the construction zone so we less frequently banged our knees in the dark.

It authenticated both our pain and the tension in our marriage, a tension we'd already learned to navigate more carefully, but could now navigate with a refreshing level of understanding and respect.

Love and commitment had kept us together. Respect for each other had carried us through the miserable days when our approaches seemed like two freight trains on the same track in a dark tunnel, barreling toward a single destination from opposite directions.

Now we adjusted our position, our posture. We'd been holding those two tensions in awkward balance—having and not having our son the way we once had. Stepping back a pace, we could see the other losses from that perspective too. Having and not having the family dynamic we'd cherished with our other children. Having and not having the freedom to be spontaneous. Having and not having weekends, long-held dreams, and impact in our professional roles.

I looked at Pat differently. He didn't hold an *opposing* view; he held the other side of the tension of having and not having. He naturally gravitated toward focusing on the "have" part of ambiguous loss. For a thousand reasons—some I was still exploring—I naturally gravitated toward the "have not" reality. And that's the nature of ambiguous loss.

The search to authenticate our experience had taken so long, too long. My soul bled for others facing their own ambiguous loss without knowing it had a name, because knowing its name and its unique dynamics could shed light on their pain.

We weren't suddenly healed. But we were healing.

Pat

Before Zach's fall and the additional surgeries, Tammy and I had learned to respect if not embrace each other's approaches to Zach's simultaneous presence and absence. So much of that new understanding was implemented as we dealt with this new threat—Zach was permanently disabled and would likely live out the rest of his life advancing no further than his current state. This palpable grief-truce enabled us to maneuver through the minefield of a new, less hopeful prognosis for Zach's future.

Culture pushes us to avoid discomfort. After Zach's injury, our family knew little else. This fresh blow was as hard to take as any of the others, but it had the word *permanence* attached to it. And yet that permanence was ambiguous in Zach's case.

Medical, religious, and legal experts rarely address ambiguous loss. Friends and relatives are usually unaware such a phenomenon exists. The devastation caused by unresolved grief only grows if it isn't acknowledged. As Tammy had discovered in Pauline Boss's material, and as we had witnessed day after day, with no supporting rituals—like a funeral for the death of a loved one—"families of the physically or psychologically missing are [often] left to fend for themselves."

We had each other, and the knowledge that even this chapter of our story was somehow melding with that larger story God was writing. We saw His hand at work providing a future home for Zach. And we understood that it was the ambiguity—not the events themselves—that intensified our discomfort.

We recognized it now. It didn't make our journey danger-free. But it did make us aware. Alert to each other's trigger moments. Sympathetic to each other's cause.

And if life ever settled down, we were determined to help other people discover that their shapeless loss had a name.

CHAPTER

17

Tammy

Embedded in the *ambiguity* of ambiguous loss is the absence of a traditional ceremony of mourning. Other people mark a funeral as a point in time when they acknowledge their grief and remember their loved one, surrounded by caring friends and family. The spouse of an Alzheimer's patient or stroke victim, a military veteran missing a limb, the parent of a kidnapped-and-still-missing child have no marker.

I needed to let go of the Zach I'd known and embrace Zach as he is today. I needed a time to mourn with others who knew and loved him. Alone in my room one day, I had repeated, "Good-bye, old Zach. Hello, new Zach. Good-bye, old Zach. Hello, new Zach." But I needed more.

While on a personal retreat with Pat, I carefully floated the idea of conducting a tribute to Zach with a few friends and family on the anniversary of Zach's injury.

Not surprisingly, Pat countered with something that would not just mourn the Zach we lost but celebrate the Zach we still have. Together, we decided to do two events on the day between the anniversary of his injury and his birthday. To symbolize the inherent tension in ambiguous loss—living with joy and sorrow together—the first would mourn losses and the second would celebrate the gift of Zach as he is now.

Pat

In preparation for the two ceremonies, I worked on two videos—one for each event—that combined pictures and video of Zach's life leading up to and after his injuries with his favorite music as accompaniment. My hope had been that the visuals would help connect attendees with the concepts of both loss and life. I couldn't have imagined the effect it would have on our son Nate.

On a normal day, Nate announced his arrival home long before he walked through our door. If we didn't hear him walking up the sidewalk singing or laughing, we'd hear him climbing the stairs with his "made-for-stage" voice broadcasting into his ever-present phone something that sounded more like stand-up comedy than it did a conversation with a friend.

But this was not a normal day.

The subdued, but still melodic "I'm home!" announcement brought Soren, Tammy, and me from our separate rooms to the kitchen. Nate was back from college. The fun had arrived.

We hugged it out with our most affectionate child, who wasted no time filling our kitchen with laughter as he recounted his most recent adventure on the Megabus ride from Philadelphia.

When our kitchen conversation turned to the events that had brought Nate home for the weekend—the ceremonies—I offered the boys the opportunity to be the first to view the technological creation I'd finished minutes before Nate walked in the door.

Creating the videos had been a profoundly cathartic experience for me. Lingering over pictures and videos of Zach prior to his accident created a space for me to acknowledge and grieve certain aspects of Zach that had been lost, aspects I—and others—desperately missed. In the process, I realized I had been in denial about many of those losses. I didn't like going there when Tammy wanted me to. It made me sad. But the longer I found myself in that space, rummaging through pictures, listening to his music, replaying special memories of Zach as he had been, the more I felt like I was flushing something out of me that had poisoned my soul and was toxic to my relationship with Tammy.

I suppose I expected it to have a slightly similar but far less intense effect on my family and our friends who would watch it the next day, but I was not prepared for Nate's reaction.

A couple of minutes into the video, a picture of Nate and Zach appeared on the screen. It was a shot I'd taken the day after an epic New England blizzard. The storm dumped so much snow in Boston that I could stand on top of a drift and boost the boys onto the roof of a nearby building.

Nate and Zach had taken turns sledding down and off the

roof and into the huge snowdrift below. The close-up snapshot captured Nate landing on top of Zach. The picture of them smiling at each other, face-to-face, with noses almost touching, sent Nate over the edge. He abruptly pushed back the chair and ran out of the room.

Tammy immediately followed. Soren and I looked at each other. Communicating without words, we agreed. *Let's give them space.* When the video ended, we found Nate lying on his bed with Tammy lying behind him, holding him in her arms. I overheard Nate, still sobbing, say, "I'm so sorry, Mom. I didn't get it. You lost your son."

Tammy avoided reveling in a confession that I suspect she had longed for, from all of us, a confession that validated the pain she had openly and consciously grieved for years. "It's okay, Nate. I'm sorry that you not only lost a brother. You lost your mom, when you needed her most."

Before the next day's ceremonies, our communal grieving of an ambiguous loss had begun.

Tammy

We took the title of both ceremonies from Ecclesiastes 3:4, "A time to mourn and a time to dance." Zach wasn't at the first ceremony—A Time to Mourn. As friends and family entered the 127-year-old brownstone church on the edge of the Harvard campus, sunlight poured through multicolored stained-glass windows.

As they arrived, guests received a program with a cover showing a picture of Zach holding two South African orphans in his arms. They filed past four tables we'd set up in the side room of the historic church. Each table contained items we'd collected that symbolized a part of Zach we had lost.

The *Lover of God* table held his pre-injury journals, his guitar, and some of his artwork, showing the intimacy of his walk with Christ. The *Outdoor Adventurer* table held the surfboard he'd once used, his infamous paintball gun, biking gloves, and fishing gear. The *Lover of Sport* table held all of his football, lacrosse, and basketball gear as well as pictures of him with his various teams. The Zach before his injury.

The last table overflowed with banners, posters, cards, and gifts people had sent throughout the years to encourage Zach and our family.

The guests were seated in the sanctuary and welcomed by one of Pat's best friends and campus minister with Cru at Stanford, Ron Sanders. Together, we watched the video of Zach's life from birth until his injury at sixteen, accompanied by Zach's favorite songs. As a mother might during a son's eulogy, I used some of his belongings to share what I missed most about Zach. Watching him move gracefully on athletic fields and do crazy mountain bike or waterskiing maneuvers, joining in as he laughed with family and friends, playing guitar and singing with him . . .

Most of all, I told the guests I missed hearing his voice— his prayers, thoughts, dreams. I missed hearing him ask how I was doing, affirming and encouraging me more as his sister in Christ than as his mother.

Each of our children spoke. Chelsea said,

Today, in this space, I would like to share feelings of grief, resentment, and guilt that often have supremely outweighed happy and grateful moments—grief for losing my eldest brother, my partner in crime, my co-student during our homeschool days, one of my best friends, who left a Zach-size hole in my heart; resentment to God for not only letting this happen, but for doing it at a time when I was already so vulnerable; guilt for being away from my family during a catastrophic loss, for being away from Zach when he was airlifted from a football field, for worrying about papers, field hockey games, making new friends, and having fun when Zach was worrying about living another day.

Guilt for trying to forget.

Guilt for not visiting Zach often enough or not doing enough to help him, stimulate his brain, engage him in activities to help him stay sharp or still feel valued and cared for by his loved ones.

Guilt for having been given a good and healthy life, body, and brain—all things Zach has lost.

It's hard to explain what it's like to lose a brother. Not really lose him, but to lose him as he used to be. I felt the sting of losing Zach every day. I felt it every time I would call his voice mail so I could hear his voice, until eventually his phone plan was cancelled.

I felt the loss every time one of my college friends brought a brother for a campus visit, took him to parties, showed him how awesome her college experience was . . . every time I desperately wanted to text Zach to reference something I knew he'd find funny, or something that reminded me of him, or a song I knew he'd love.

I still feel it every time I have to explain his situation to a new friend or acquaintance who asks about my siblings—where they went to college, what they're doing now—every time I realize someone precious to me, like a college friend, never got to meet Zach as he was before.

They never knew him.

It's a pain that lingers. It's messy, it doesn't have a clear beginning or end, and I feel it with every breath. I ache to have Zach as he was.

Nate continued in the same vein:

I remember, in the years before I left for college, the endless struggle with grief and ambiguous loss. Right when the wounds of sorrow would seem to heal, they would be torn open again by a tired look I saw on my dad's face or the sounds of crying I heard from my mother's bedroom.

It's as impossible as it is useless to deny the grief that was caused by this incident. Simply put, when I was in eighth grade I lost my brother to a coma and my sister to college. I watched my father drown in a sea of paperwork and hospital bills and my mother drown in a pool of tears. Eight years ago, Zach wrote down a list of ten things he appreciated about me. I didn't respond at the time. Here are my ten things— almost eight years too late—that I love and miss about Zach:

1. I miss his voice.
2. I miss his writing.
3. I miss watching him treat our mom with love and respect, and I wish he had been there to make me treat her better.
4. I miss having a role model and friend.
5. I miss having a teacher and mentor.
6. I miss watching him and Soren fall asleep snuggling, and I miss being jealous of that but too prideful to join in.
7. I miss his strong, capable body.
8. I love his tender heart.
9. I love his endless generosity.
10. I love knowing that he would lay down his life for me, his brother.

But now it's time to let go.

Soren didn't want to speak. At the last minute he decided to read a poem he had written two years into our grief journey, referring to a huge pillow he and Zach used when they shared the same bed.

THE PILLOW

A pillow is a
soft,
rectangular
object used to
sleep,
but my pillow

contains
something more.
My pillow
represents a relationship between you and me,
     my brother.
We shared that
extra-long
plush pillow
when I was just
a baby.
You would hold
me in your hands
every night
and we would
rest our heads
on that pillow.
Even though I
could not
speak, you knew
I appreciated you.

Hearing the expressions of my children's losses touched me deeply and reminded me that the ceremony held value, purpose, and promise.

Guests were given blue cards and a time of silence during which they could record the things they missed about Zach. After the silence, several friends stood and shared what they had written.

I had learned that people who suffer a severe traumatic brain injury lose all their friends within a year. But Zach's friends didn't forget about him, even after they graduated and went to college or started jobs. They still journey with him.

Pat spoke last about God's nearness in suffering and thanked everyone for all they had done for our family. We played the song I wrote for Zach, "Beauty in Suffering," during a second slideshow with pictures of Zach's recovery.

In closing, we prayed together a "Litany of Ambiguous Loss" written by Ron Sanders.

Today we pray for Zach, his family, and his friends.
We pray for those who care for him and those he will touch.

For Zach's love for family and friends
and for those on the margins,

All: We give thanks.

For Zach's mischievous streak,

All: We give thanks.

For Zach's ability to turn a compliment
back on the person who gave it,

All: We give thanks.

For Zach's athletic ability and his love of sport—
the games, his teammates, and his coaches,

All: We give thanks.

For the depth of Zach's love for Christ
demonstrated in worship, prayer, and service,

All: We give thanks.

For memories made and lost,

All: Lord, have mercy.

For words that must now go unsaid,

All: Lord, have mercy.

For relationships that have changed—
family and friends,

All: Lord, have mercy.

For lost hopes and shattered dreams,

All: Lord, have mercy.

For our worries and fears for Zach
and the McLeod family,

All: Lord, have mercy.

For the abiding presence of Christ in suffering,

All: Thanks be to God.

For the profound spiritual presence and
deep joy evident in Zach after his accident,

All: Thanks be to God.

For the incredible medical staff and
those hidden moments that have kept Zach alive,

All: Thanks be to God.

For Zach's ability to lift others with a smile, hug, thumbs up,
high five, or secret handshake that only he knows,

All: Thanks be to God.

Now, may the God who suffers with us in our weakness,
who dries our tears with promise,
and who is able to offer hope in our despair
take care of you, watch over you, and give you grace.

All: Amen.

We invited people to leave the cards on which they'd recorded their losses in an oversized bottle as they exited, reflecting Psalm 56:8 which tells us, "You [God] have collected all my tears in your bottle" (NLT).

This was the community of people who carried us. Many cried with us. Some said they were unaware how much they needed this type of ceremony, and the power of a communal experience of acknowledging losses, griefs, guilt, and our togetherness in it.

Having grieved in community, I left the church with a lighter heart.

The second ceremony, A Time to Dance, was a birthday celebration for Zach at the historic Cambridge Boat Club on the Charles River, right across the street from Zach's high school. A friend had volunteered to rent the boathouse for us, a spot that was convenient for our guests—just a two-minute drive from the church—and meaningful to me because of its view of the river along which I'd run and started rowing in order to enter Nate's world. Even the room itself showed the contrast between the two ceremonies—the boat club light and airy compared to the dark wood paneling of the side room at the historic church.

Zach attended that celebration ceremony, elated to see all his friends gathered in one place.

We watched the slideshow of Zach's post-injury pictures that captured significant milestones in his recovery and expressed Zach as he is now. We invited guests to write affirmations about Zach on gold cards and to share them at the microphone if they desired. Many came forward to affirm Zach and tell him what they appreciated about him. Others added humorous stories, some of which were new to us—girls who wanted to marry him and antics on a high school camping trip. Zach, as expected, grinned through it all and hugged each speaker.

More than a birthday party, it was a celebration of life.

Earlier I'd wondered if it might be difficult to transition from the ceremony of ambiguous loss to the birthday party. It wasn't. I cried during the ceremony but laughed at the party. And, yes, I danced. I danced with Zach. I danced with the community who'd carried me through years of mourning. Most importantly, I danced with Pat.

Pauline Boss was right. The secret to living well with ambiguous loss requires living well with both having and not having someone the way you once had them.

Both grieving and celebrating in community helped me make a much-needed turn, helped our family make the turn, and helped Pat and me make a significant turn.

I keep a few of Zach's mementos from that day in a special container under my bed. I pull it out once in a while and am reminded of the ambivalence of this loss—that as Ecclesiastes says, I can experience simultaneously "a time to mourn and a time to dance."

Pat

The rituals Tammy needed provided hope for all of us. We embraced the ambiguity of both having and not having Zach. Publicly rather than privately. Corporately rather than individually. Communally rather than in isolation.

Something happened to our marriage as we together created and stood side by side through the ceremony of loss and the celebration of life.

Our individual versions of grief melded into one.

CHAPTER

18

Pat

Ambiguous loss will probably always remain part of our family's legacy. It will move in and out of the forefront, but never completely disappear. Like mountain hikers, we're learning how to cinch our backpack straps tighter, adjust the weight so it doesn't rub on already stressed spots, and keep climbing.

Ambiguous disappointment often accompanies ambiguous loss. For so long, we disappointed each other—drawing close when the other needed space, keeping our distance when the other needed closeness, misreading each other's cues about whether an incident was comedic or catastrophic in the other's opinion, misjudging which of our children needed us most at any given moment. I clung to the gains Zach made as a survival technique. Tammy felt pummeled by what could be no more. I suspect she might have said that it seemed dishonoring to Zach and to the whole process not to acknowledge what was gone.

Before we were plunged into the world of ambiguous loss, our marriage could have been described as a team effort. We were on a mission to build our family and help change the world. If pressed to choose a one-word description for it, I would choose *companionship*. In the months following Zach's injury on the football field and the subsequent trauma-drama, we operated as an efficient crisis management team. Two years after the incident, our relationship was marked by tension, exhaustion, and the emotional disconnect of grieving differently.

But we contended for our marriage and reclaimed companionship and respect. We allowed each other the gift of separate approaches to the same crisis. We leaned on the wisdom of godly counselors who could think clearly when we were caught in a tangle of unsolvables.

Even today, I mourn the years we'll never get back with our other children when we were so engrossed in Zach's care. We did what we had to do. We included our children in hospital visits and care responsibilities—which sometimes backfired in the "togetherness" effort—but no one could deny that circumstances changed their childhoods, changed Chelsea's college experience. How could any young person not resent the interruptions and intrusions, the upheaval?

Nate never seemed to tire of Zach's presence in our apartment, although it was difficult for everyone.

I caught a glimpse of how deeply Soren had been affected when I read a sobering piece of verse he'd written:

When I look into Zach's eyes, I see courage,
But I also see how worn out he looks
And how much pain he has gone through.
I don't want to, but I think about
How much easier it would have been for him
If he had passed away.

Soren eventually revised his own attachment to Zach after a basketball injury landed Soren in the office of a physical therapist. His quick recovery from the nagging injury inspired him to start taking Zach to physical therapy appointments each week and work more closely with Zach in his own rehabilitation efforts. By switching roles with Zach and becoming his coach, physically, Soren resurrected Zach's role in his life as a spiritual coach and role model.

The ironies compounded daily interest. Tammy and I were cleaning up after a personal hygiene accident one moment and being interviewed on the national stage the next, installing safety rails in a century-old Victorian home and then immediately diving into the public spotlight on the national concussion debate. Reaching out to children with disabilities in South Africa, only to find one in our family circle.

Curiously, some of the qualities the game of football developed in me helped sustain me through our ambiguous loss. Choosing to live with determination, a positive attitude, hard work, and dedication; focusing on what I could control and not getting mired in what I couldn't; pushing through adversity; overcoming obstacles; celebrating the underdog story . . .

I've aged a lot since Zach was injured. Tammy says she sees it in my face—an unending fatigue. The process of figuring out how to live within my own limits is ongoing. I'm embracing rest more often and better understanding the rhythms of parenting an adult child with brain trauma. And I'm accepting that Tammy and I are wired differently on purpose.

People occasionally approach me after sporting events or church and tell me, "I love watching the way you and your family interact" or "It's like a sermon by itself." It becomes clear in the conversation that follows that what they really mean is they love watching Zach interact with us. They find his unfiltered enthusiasm and public displays of affection mesmerizing, or they love watching him worship. I don't blame them. So do I.

I hope such a comment will apply to our marriage and family more broadly every year. The truth is that after nearly four decades of marriage and more than ten years of wrestling with ambiguous loss, Tammy and I are still adjusting to each other's movements across the dance floor of life. The stutter steps. The turns. The dips, the distance, the times when we seem to be listening to two different songs, or when both try to lead and neither wants to follow. But we are learning, making progress, and perhaps more than ever before being gentle with each other.

Tammy

Ambiguous loss is by nature undefinable. I saw it at work in our family, and I now understand why so many couples disintegrate in the acid rain of ambiguous loss. We might have been among them if we hadn't considered our commitment to each other nonnegotiable, even when we stood on opposite sides of ongoing debates. We held tightly to what we had in common—love for Zach, love for our other children, love for and devotion to God, who taught us that suffering is not without purpose or reward.

I still mourn the repercussions of ambiguous loss in Soren's, Nate's, and Chelsea's lives. I was there for them, but not fully there. I listened to their growing pains, but they knew I had one ear tuned to the "child" who could not fend for himself. I loved them, but as any mother would, I wondered if my expressions of love matched what their hearts most needed.

Again, Nicholas Wolterstorff's *Lament for a Son* helped me find language for what we were experiencing: "We don't just each have a gap inside us but together a gap among us. We have to live differently with each other. We have to live around the gap. Pull one out, and everything changes."

Until recently, Chelsea lived nearby. We enjoyed having our adult daughter close enough to share impromptu lunches and dinners, relying on her tips about the trendiest and healthiest eateries in the Boston area. We still carry on long conversations about life, work, and friends.

During the time that Chelsea worked for Sports Legacy Institute (now Concussion Legacy Foundation) after college, she dove deeper into the intersection of sports and concussions' aftereffects. She offered to create a website for Zach in her off hours to keep his friends updated.

She lived at home during several of the summers when Zach was there on weekends. It was obvious that seeing him so different from what he'd been—and been to her—took a toll. The dynamic of their relationship naturally changed.

We're watching Soren and Nate pursue their dreams with the requisite losses and gains, successes and direction-altering disappointments. We've followed Nate's screenwriting and act-ing talents to Scotland and Los Angeles, and we see Soren step-ping into adulthood with confidence.

Pat had told me he thought his role had been to absorb part of the loss for us, part of the pain. But together, we strength-ened our ability to absorb loss. As Jerry Sittser writes in *A Grace Disguised: How the Soul Grows through Loss*, "I did not get over the loss of my loved ones; rather, I absorbed the loss into my life, like soil receives decaying matter, until it became a part of who I am."

My lowest moments in the journey were the times when it was obvious Zach's injury stirred a firestorm of relational fallout—with our kids, or between Pat and me. My heart broke when my kids would tell me to stop being sad. As if I could. And to stop making everything about Zach. What child wouldn't feel that way? The fact that I couldn't undo what hap-pened to Zach and how it affected them still burdens me.

Coming to terms with the loss of verbal communication Zach and I used to enjoy was a puzzle piece I finally put in place, helping me validate the ocean-floor depth of my early sense of loss.

Determination, dedication, and hard work served us both well as we embarked on this journey and as we keep moving forward on an unending marathon. Like Pat, I need reminders about my limits and the importance of recharging. For me, refueling still comes through solitude, silence, prayer, reflec-tion, nature, beauty, music, good connections with family and friends, and time in Scripture.

I have come to understand the value of lament—an over-looked practice in modern life but quite common in the Bible.

When I read the psalmists' laments laced with praise, I'm encouraged by God's nearness in our pain.

He did not hover, disinterested, outside or above the hospital building, the rehab center, the May Center School, or our home. He entered *into* our pain with us. I found that truth indescribably healing.

One of my most treasured examples of Zach's unwavering faith—despite how different his life looks from what any of us imagined—is also one of the clearest pictures of God's presence in our pain. I stand behind Zach, trying to keep him from hugging everyone while he holds the plate of bread for the people who come forward to receive Communion at our church on Sunday evenings. It is my role to say to each person moving through the line, "The body of Christ, broken for you."

But one night, he interrupted me after "The body of Christ . . ." In his unique way of vocalizing, he added, "broken for you." It's now our pattern every time we serve Communion.

Yes, Zach. Broken for you. And for me.

CHAPTER

19

Tammy

Zach and I were enjoying the evening together in a Jacuzzi on the back porch of our friends' home in Florida. It was spring break—a needed respite from work and school responsibilities. The night sky was ablaze with an expanse of stars over the ocean.

Zach seemed lost in the stars. I asked him, "What are you thinking about, Zach?"

In a faint and gravelly voice, he laboriously answered, "My beau . . . ti . . . ful Fa . . . ther in hea . . . ven."

I had always relished hearing Zach's voice—whether he was giving speeches so moving they made people cry, or telling me about his adventures as we washed dishes together, or saying his prayers at night, or just asking me how I was doing. He spoke his ideas openly and without hesitation.

Today Zach can barely speak, but he understands everything we say. He listens, prays, and speaks with his eyes and facial expressions, even if words are hard to express.

It's evident his mind is active with profound thoughts. He enjoys life with the exuberance of a young child and the reckless abandonment of the present moment, not dwelling on the regrets of three minutes ago or the threats of three minutes into the future.

Four days a week Zach attends Boston University's Intensive Cognitive-Communication Rehabilitation program. ICCR is an intensive speech and language therapy program for young adults with brain injury who are interested in continuing or pursuing secondary education. He has four classroom-style lectures with individual and group therapy daily.

He's still making the news. The cover of a magazine featured Zach in his life vest in a two-person racing shell, with his perpetually smiling face turned toward the sun as he and his adaptive instructor sculled on the Charles River. The *Boston Globe* recently featured his volunteering efforts for his high school's athletic department and the role he now plays as a permanent motivational presence on the field and in the locker room.

One of my favorite photographs of Zach was taken at the beginning of a high school football game. Two hulking football players are holding Zach up as the three of them step onto that familiar playing field. Zach's gait isn't smooth like theirs. His posture lists to one side. He's dressed in the team uniform, although he doesn't wear shoulder pads, knee pads, or a helmet. He isn't playing, but he is part of the team. The same Friday night lights shine down on him. An even more intense light shines *out* of him to others, including the teammates bracing him on either side.

He belongs. He's a leader in his own way. As younger players grow up around him and move on in life, he remains. I once struggled with that reality, but no longer. The role Zach serves is vital to the health of the team, the entire community. And the example he sets by showing up and rising from every hard hit of life reveals he's asking—in a more significant way—"Coach, put me in the game."

And He does.

Two years ago, during a devotional time with him, I asked Zach the given question for the day: "What do you thirst for?"

He typed on his iPad, "I thirst for God because He has given me life and joy. I will keep on worshiping Him as long as I live."

Zach's focus today is the same as what he journaled the month before his injury.

He speaks and teaches me through his love-filled actions—prompting me not to rush mealtime prayers by keeping his head lowered and not letting go of my hand . . . constantly signing "thank you" . . . giving spontaneous hugs and high fives to strangers in doctors' offices, elevators, and on the street . . . approaching people others don't see—especially those with disabilities, the homeless, the lonely, the brokenhearted—and giving them a tender touch . . . asking people if they are doing all right and allowing them freedom to admit when they are not . . . gently putting his hand on my shoulder when I am having a difficult day.

Engaging with Zach has offered me inner renewal. His life and faith, his exuberance and deep sense of caring, make me consider my own actions, pursuits, and goals with renewed perspective. Much as Henri Nouwen observed in his book *Adam: God's Beloved*, I'm finding in my son "a presence and a safe space to recognize and accept [my] own, often invisible disabilities." At first, I saw only his disabilities, his limitations. But the more time I've spent with Zach, the more I've realized my own. Many times I've wondered, *Who is the disabled one here?* The boundaries are less clear.

If what makes us most human is our ability to love God and people, then I would say I know of few people who are more human or live out their purpose in life of glorifying God more than Zach.

Pat

In mid-April of 2013, I was seated on a platform in front of a couple of hundred professors and campus ministers in the Harvard Club of New York City, preparing to give a short speech in response to an academic paper being read by a philosophy professor. I'd come to New York with more emotional exhaustion than ever, a reminder that ambiguous loss returns in waves. When I finished my speech and handed the microphone back, I sat in my assigned chair with a sigh of relief that my modest contribution to the event was done.

But during the question-and-answer time, I was pulled back into the conversation. A person from the audience asked the main speaker, "How do you, as a Christian professor, respond to the problem of evil, death, and suffering in a world supposedly created by a loving and all-powerful God?"

The speaker gave a solid answer, similar to how I'd often responded to the same question—before the hard hit call, before the twelve-foot fall, and before the Boston Marathon bombing just days earlier. But the professor's answer was not the one that came to my mind in that moment.

Instead, my mind drifted over the traumatic events our family had lived through in the previous years, along with a scene from the week before. Minutes after the first frantic news reports came out about a bombing that had killed and injured dozens of marathoners and bystanders, I came to the horrible realization that I hadn't yet heard from Soren, who had gone with friends to watch the runners near the finish line.

When a text message finally made its way through the over-loaded cell phone network—"Dad, I'm okay"—my body went limp.

I now realized that, in difficult situations, I often brace myself to prepare for the worst possible news. Yet more than that has changed—the way I view suffering has changed as well. I knew I had something to add to this conversation at the New York City Harvard Club.

So I responded out of character. After the professor finished answering the question, I raised my hand and said, "I wonder if I might offer a response." He graciously handed me the mic.

I faced the audience. "Recently, I have developed a different perspective on the problem of evil and suffering than the one I used to have. Far from thinking of suffering as the 'rock of atheism'—as the unassailable argument against the existence of a loving and powerful God—I have come to believe that the Christian response to evil and suffering may, in fact, be one of the most compelling arguments *for* the Christian faith.

"It is the answer that came to me in November when my wife was diagnosed with cancer, and in December when my son, who had already suffered one traumatic brain injury that left him permanently disabled, suffered a second traumatic brain injury. And in January when I was going back and forth between hospitals to see my wife who had just come out of surgery and my son who was recovering from brain surgery. And in February when I was visiting my dad who was nearing the end of his battle with cancer and received a call informing me that our youngest son, Soren, had suffered a concussion playing basketball. And if that were not enough, now, in April, as Boston begins emerging from one of the most bizarre weeks of senseless terror in the city's history."

I watched the faces in the room react. Even if they hadn't been moved by our personal traumas, the whole world had been rocked by what had happened in Boston.

"A week ago, on the night after the bombing, I was unable to fall asleep. Soren had been across the street from the second bomb when it exploded. He wasn't injured physically, but we are still calculating the impact on his soul. Since I was restless that night, I assumed he was too. I tapped on his bedroom door and opened it quietly. Out of the darkness I heard, 'What's up, Dad?'

"I said, 'Want to pray?'

"'Sure.'

"We knelt together in that dark room, and something happened. I still don't have words to describe the peace and calm that came over me as these thoughts went through my mind and came out of my mouth: 'God, it gives my heart great consolation knowing that right now we are kneeling before a crucified God. You are not a god who cannot sympathize with our experiences of pain, death, and suffering. You are the God who came into this world, who suffered, and who died in order to save us forever from a world that is filled with evil and suffering.'"

Tammy

One of Jerry Sittser's quotes I have leaned on through this journey is this:

> The experience of loss does not have to leave us with
> the memory of a painful event that stands alone, like a
> towering monument that dominates the landscape of
> our lives. Loss can also leave us with the memory of a
> wonderful story. It can function as a catalyst that pushes
> us in a new direction, like a closed road that forces us to
> turn around and find another way to our destination.
> Who knows what we will discover and see along the way?
> The suffering my children, family, friends, and
> I have experienced is part of an ongoing story that is still
> being written. . . . The loss was not simply the ending of
> something good; it was also the beginning of something
> else. And that has turned out to be good, too.

In fact, I'm viewing restoration differently these days. I'd hoped Zach and I would one day pick up where we'd left off, playing our guitars together and singing. We do still play and sing at church twice a year, and some Sundays at home when he's with us. But we're not facing each other, as we once did, or sitting side by side in the same way.

Because Zach can play only with his left hand, fingering the chords, I reach over the body of his guitar and strum. I sing. Sometimes Zach will try to add a vocal word or two. He alternates between focusing on the music, turning his attention to smiling broadly at the congregation, and closing his eyes in worship.

Worshiping together was restored. Not as I expected or

hoped. But as we—in our unique pairing—played and sang "What a Beautiful Name" during a recent church service, I sensed my heart shifting to embrace a revised expectation, a new but rewarding way of connecting with my son and with our shared love for God.

I took one author's suggestion to heart to create a list of the good that has come from our family's version of ambiguous loss. Once I began keeping a list of what I've learned, I found myself adding to it regularly. As the entries grew, I could feel my soul expanding.

What I learned about grief and loss:
- How to grieve.
- To understand people's suffering more.
- Grief can isolate because people grieve in different ways and on different timetables.
- Many people don't "do sorrow" well.
- Many don't know how to grieve.
- Catastrophic loss taxes marriage.
- In times of grief, we have to be gentle with each other in order to preserve close relationships.
- People want to help in times of catastrophic loss.

What I learned about myself:
- I will be okay even if horrible things happen to me.
- I can be well even if I have to do a lot of things I don't like to do.
- I need to do some life-giving things to endure the things that are life-draining.
- How to receive help.

- How important it is to tell people how I am really doing.
- It is good to keep working during catastrophic loss and not collapse on the injured person.
- How much a spiritual connection adds to a close relationship.
- I need encouragement from God.
- I need to engage in physical activity to be able to endure suffering.
- I need to be in nature to expand my horizons and to be renewed, refreshed, equipped to endure suffering.
- I will be okay even if I am in a lot of pain.
- I can face pain and not run from it.
- My only true hope is in God and His Word.
- I am not in control of anything except my choices.
- I will be okay if I don't get what I want.
- I have developed a more robust theology of the problem of evil and suffering.

What I learned about disability:
- Living with severe disability in the family is difficult.
- Living with severe disability in the family is neither comfortable nor convenient.
- People with disabilities have a powerful effect on other people's lives.

What I learned about suffering:
- It is God's nature to be near us in suffering.
- God weeps over our anguish.

- Joy and happiness are two different things.
- Suffering deeply impacts communities and individuals.
- People aren't comfortable when things don't turn out well (i.e., when miraculous healing doesn't occur).
- Lament is important but seldom practiced. We rarely encourage it in ourselves or others.
- It is good to just sit in silence when suffering.
- A person can communicate with another even in silence.
- People who have everything go well for them don't really "get" suffering.

What I learned about God:
- God helps people endure horrible things.
- God doesn't always answer yes when we ask for a respite, but He will not break a bruised reed nor quench a smoldering wick (Isaiah 42:3).
- God can help us even if we don't get a reprieve—He gives strength to the weary.
- God is good even if He doesn't physically heal those who are suffering.
- God's Word speaks loudly to those who are in pain.
- God's presence is enough.

The list is still growing. Among the entries that mean the most to me is this one:

- Learning what a great dad Pat is. Some dads take off when life gets hard.

Pat

Today we live in that redeemed ambiguity—incredible suffering and incredible love in the same messy world.

After we'd enjoyed a movie downtown together one night, I suggested that Tammy, Chelsea, Nate, and Soren ride in Chelsea's car, which was parked closest to the theater. Zach and I would take our car, which was farther down the street on the third floor of a parking garage.

Zach likely detected the competition implied in this arrangement. *Who will get home first?* Like a racehorse when the gate opens, Zach took off. I grabbed the gait belt he wears around his midsection and held on—feeling more like a bull rider in a rodeo than a jockey with a racehorse.

We quickly outpaced the crowd of people moving down the sidewalk. Then suddenly, Zach stopped and spun me around. Bending over, he took notice of the person everyone else had ignored, including me. He locked eyes with the homeless man who sat on a piece of cardboard on the sidewalk, holding a cup with a few coins in it. Zach reached out his hand and gave the man a high five. Neither said a word, but several gigabytes of data passed between them as they stared and smiled at each other. Download complete, Zach turned and started trotting again.

We reached the garage and still had a good hike ahead of us—about the length of a football field and up a long ramp. Zach—with his enduring enthusiasm and unsteady gait— seemed to view the challenge before us as if he were about to receive a kickoff and run it back for a touchdown. Without looking back at me, he leaned forward and started *charging* up the hill. He pulled me along as if I were a defensive player trying to keep him from getting away.

"Zach, slow down," I said, laughing as I held on. When I realized I wasn't going to be able to stop him, I said, "Zach, when I grow up I want to be like you."

His gallop slowed as he processed what I had just said, glancing briefly at me with a look that asked, *What are you talking about?* Then he turned his attention back to the car he could now see at the top of the ramp.

Between gasps for breath, I said, "I want to embrace the challenges of life with enthusiasm, the way you do."

Shaking his head, Zach kept trotting and I kept talking.

"I want to notice people the way you notice people. I want to light up peoples' faces the way you light up faces. I want to see the people who are invisible to those in positions of power and privilege."

Zach kept his eyes on the goal.

Breathing even harder, I said, "I want to step into each moment and be present with people and not be distracted by memories of the past or worries about the future. I want to notice when people are upset, or concerned, or distraught—the way you notice them."

As the pace and volume of my comments picked up, his stride slowed more.

"I want to leave a trail of smiles behind me when I walk out of a room. I want to pray without ceasing and give thanks in everything. I want to radiate joy from the moment I open my eyes each morning until the moment my head hits the pillow each night. I want to be able to make people feel loved the way you make them feel loved. When I grow up, I want to be like you, Zach."

I wasn't finished. There was more I wanted to say. Zach crossed the goal line and stopped at the car. Turning around, he grabbed me, and with impressive strength pulled me into his embrace—an embrace that clearly said he had no intention of letting go. I didn't want him to.

For that eternal moment—a moment I will never stop replaying in my mind, a moment that we relive in person every time we are together and hold each other—for at least that one brief moment, everything in our universe seemed right again.

> *The rest of my life, however short, however long,*
> *I know I can rejoice daily,*
> *because Christ's love and His power are there,*
> *and my calling now is simply to live for Christ's glory,*
> *and to just let Him flow through my broken heart.*
>
> ZACH MCLEOD
>
> (quote from his baptismal testimony two weeks before his injury)

Every photo before Zach's hard hit carries weight, as if the image were imprinted on stone. Each reveals a vibrant child, an active young person now locked in time and memory for us. The images of Zach after his injury and surgeries tell another story. Initially, they show him stripped of strength, vitality, and the light that had always shone from his eyes. Even though he didn't—and likely won't—return to his pre-injury self, later pictures reveal that his vibrancy, enthusiasm, deep faith, and love for his family are not only unimpaired, but stronger than ever.

▲ Zach dressed in his childhood hero's Denver Broncos uniform, already suited up for what we all assumed his future might look like.

▲ (l. to r.) Soren (in the same uniform, following his brother's lead), Zach, and Nate—with nothing to foreshadow what lay ahead a few years later.

◀ Family photo after Pat and Tammy told the kids the family was going to South Africa that summer.

◀ Zach and Tammy enjoying a closeness that both sustained her and intensified her grief following Zach's injury.

Zach holding two children at the Sizanani orphanage in South Africa. Within two weeks, their physical and neurological needs would also be his. ▶

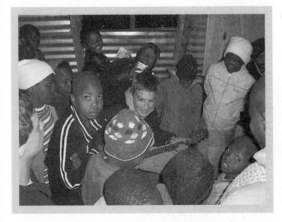

◀ Zach playing guitar for kids in a South African village. It would be one of the last times he'd strum a guitar unhindered.

Zach in a scrimmage a week before the injury that changed everything. ▶

Tammy singing to Zach the day after his injury, hoping somehow his subconscious mind—battered and bruised—could find hope in the music he'd loved. ▶

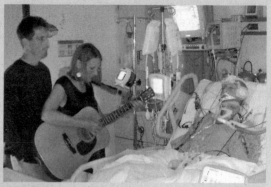

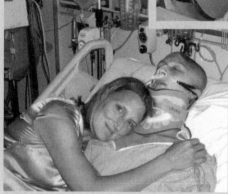

◀ Tammy with Zach after the surgery to remove his skullcap, the operation that made him more vulnerable than ever.

Zach learning to walk again with the help of a physical therapist and his "You can do this, Zach!" dad. ▶

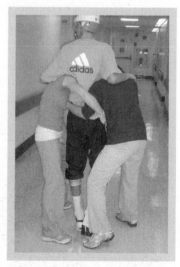

◀ Pat and Zach early in his stay at Spaulding Rehab. Pat climbed inside the protective "African tent bed" with Zach, the escape artist.

◀ Coach Papas and his son, Nico, one of Zach's teammates, visiting Zach at Spaulding Rehab, reminding him he wasn't forgotten and was still considered part of the team.

Zach and his sister, Chelsea, best friends on a new journey. ▶

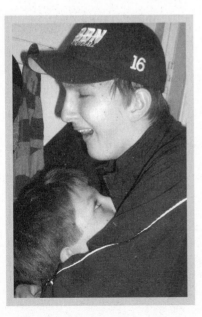

◀ Zach hugging Soren as only Zach can—with all his heart and strength.

Zach back in South Africa, serving others despite his challenges, doing what he does best—sharing the love of Christ with whoever's in reach. ▶

◀ Celebrating with his classmates at their high school graduation, where Zach received an honorary certificate.

▲ Meeting Tim Tebow—two football players inspiring each other.

Zach and Nate on the field at Gillette Stadium prior to meeting Tim and his family. ▶

◄ Hugging Tim Tebow, kindred spirits with a shared desire to brighten the lives of others.

▲ Tammy praying with Zach in her study, rekindling their spiritual connection though the words were gone.

▲ Pat holding Zach after playing catch, a father gripping the son whose light still shines.

(l. to r.) Tammy, Zach, Nate, Soren, and Pat at Zach's school's homecoming game, cheering from the sidelines even though Zach had been permanently sidelined by his injury. ▶

◀ Zach and Coach Papas sharing a moment of sheer joy. Zach knows few moments that aren't.

▲ Zach bowed in prayer in Pat's home office, a posture that is not uncommon for him.

Zach cradling a football, still enjoying sports with his family and friends and more in love with life than ever. ▶

◀ One of the tribute tables at the ambiguous loss ceremony (note that for reasons unknown, Zach decided to alternate both spellings of his name the summer prior to the injury and landed on "Zach" afterward).

Tammy speaking to those gathered for the ceremony, describing how the items and messages she'd found in Zach's backpack had anchored them all to hope. ▶

◀ The blue and gold cards on which the ceremony attendees could write their thoughts about what they missed in Zach and what they celebrated about him.

Zach learning adaptive rowing on the Charles River with Community Rowing Inc. This is the same river along which Tammy ran and prayed and worshiped. ▶

▲ (l. to r.) Soren, Tammy, Zach, Chelsea, Pat, Nate—a family learning to live well with what was lost and what now is.

Zach with Tammy and Pat, facing the future with all its uncertainties, leaning on one another. ▶

◀ Zach kissing Tammy, wordlessly expressing his love for a mother who both grieved and hoped.

Acknowledgments

THE JOURNEY RECORDED within these pages has shown us that we truly are made from the material of our communal lives.

Steve and Anne, within minutes of that first dreadful phone call, you surrounded us. Over the phone, you calmly guided us to the hospital, where you stood waiting for us. You stayed with us late into the night, and you've stayed close ever since. Crucial turning points in this story occurred while we were on retreat at your cabin in the mountains of New Hampshire. Thank you.

We thank God for all of the medical professionals in Boston who helped save Zach's life and nursed him back to health. We especially thank you, Dr. Zafonte, for overseeing Zach's care for the past decade.

Thanks to Dr. Chris Nowinski and Dr. Robert Cantu, who cofounded the Concussion Legacy Foundation; to Dr. Ann McKee, Director of Boston University's Chronic Traumatic Encephalopathy (CTE) Center; and to similar research groups for raising awareness about the long-term risks of sports-related head injuries.

We also thank all of the school personnel who helped Zach recover: Cambridge Public Schools, the May Center School for Brain Injury (especially you, Stacey, for giving us hope through your personal weekly updates about Zach), and the Intensive Cognitive-Communication Rehabilitation program at Boston University. Thank you, Anastasia, for finding this program, and thank you, Dr. Kiran,

Katrina, Natalie, and Lindsey, for your cutting-edge therapy that is so desperately needed all over the world for people who have acquired brain injuries. May your tribe increase.

Department of Developmental Services, we are so humbled by and thankful for your tireless advocacy for Zach and all those who live with disabilities. Massachusetts Association for the Blind, we are so grateful for the home, community, and meaningful daily work and activities that you provide Zach.

Buckingham Browne & Nichols (high school) community, you carried us through this tragedy. Thank you, Rebecca and Jack, for your thoughtful and caring leadership. Coach Papas and the football community, we could not have made it through this crisis without you. Thanks to Eddie, Mike, and Nick for sponsoring the annual Zach McLeod 3v3 Basketball Tournament that has helped take the financial pressure off our family. To all the families who gave food, paid for cleaning and laundry services, hauled around our other children, wrote poems, gave monetary gifts or gifts of nights out, or offered empty homes where we could go for respite, we are incredibly grateful.

And to Zach's friends—where would our family be without you? Those who suffer traumatic brain injuries typically lose all their friends within one year. It's been ten years, and you are still connected to Zach. You will never know how much your initiations with our family mean to us. Your visits, calls, emails, and fund-raisers have blessed our lives beyond measure. We feel a very special bond with you and are excited to see who each of you will become and how you will serve in the world.

Park Street Church community, thanks for providing six months of meals for our family, and for all the support you gave us by listening to our stories and praying for us. Violette and Armen, Meg and Tim, and Toni and Walter, we wouldn't have made it through this trial without you. Thanks, Leslie, for the Enable Boston disability ministry that has helped make a way for Zach to continue to participate in and serve in the life of our church. And to Zach's small group, thanks for including him . . . as a peer.

Cru Boston staff and students, thanks for filling all the holes in ministry at Harvard and in Boston while we were sitting in hospitals.

And to our long-distance friends, thanks for your prayers, calls, and emails. Nancy, Spud, and Bonnie, thanks for traveling to Boston to support us and especially for your help with the ceremony of ambiguous loss. Gwill, thanks so much for hosting Zach's birthday party afterward.

Marty, thanks for always being there—even when I (Pat) tried running away. And thanks for always being right—even when I don't want to hear it. Jon, thanks for helping me in those first several weeks to process the tumultuous events of each day and converting those conversations into daily CaringBridge posts for our community of friends and family.

Our gratitude to Tim Tebow and the Tebow Foundation for your kindness to us and for all your efforts to bring joy and hope to those in difficult situations.

Brad, your counseling helped us learn to be gentle with each other. Thanks for giving us a safe place to talk about the issues that threatened our marriage and family.

Dr. Boss, thanks for all your research and writing about ambiguous loss. Your coining of the term and lifetime of service in this field have helped many, including us. We hope our story will draw even more people to your books and articles.

Dr. Adams, thanks for giving me (Tammy) the vision for and impetus to write our story in hopes that it might help others. We pray that it will.

Anna, our stories would never have come together as a book without you and your thousands of volunteer hours spent reading, editing, and training us to write our story. We are grateful for your sacrifice for us.

Janet, thanks for believing in the book, pitching the proposal to publishers, and connecting us to Cynthia. Cynthia, thank you for taking our collection of scenes and turning them into a more coherent story about ambiguous loss—and doing it without losing our unique voices. We are so grateful for the countless hours you took getting to know us, our story, and our writing, and pulling everything together. You are delightful to work with!

Thank you, Tyndale House Publishers—and especially Jillian Schlossberg, Kim Miller, and Bonne Steffen—for believing in this story and for patiently working with us to turn our story into a book.

Chelsea, Nate, and Soren, thanks to you most of all for your patience with us through this trial. We know you lost not only a brother, but a father and a mother for a while. We did so many things wrong throughout this process; we are grateful for your grace and forgiveness. Your authenticity, strength, and courage have not been lost on us. We learned from you and pray that God will somehow "restore the years the locusts have eaten" (see Joel 2:25, ESV), and give you glimpses of redemption within your own experience of ambiguous loss.

And last, thank you, God, for Your sustaining strength in tragedy. We are grateful that You are a God who "is near to the brokenhearted and saves those who are crushed in spirit" (Psalm 34:18, NASB). Thanks that You understand suffering and are with us in it. We look forward to someday seeing Zach with You in his new body and hearing him speak again. Thanks, too, for teaching us through him. We hope someday to love You and others the way that he does.

With gratitude,

Tammy and Pat McLeod

Writer's Note

from Cynthia Ruchti

THE RETELLING OF ANY TRUE STORY comes with an unspoken caveat. Some memories remain fresh and crisp years later—indelibly written on the soul and mind. Others are influenced by the trauma *in medias res*—as it happened—or shape-shift as time eases pain and reframes the experience with the advantage of hindsight.

In this retelling, we have made every effort to portray events, timelines, and scenes as accurately as possible, while spotlighting the elements deemed most important to you, the reader. Some people have been left anonymous in the book, although their influence was strong. Minor details and insignificant wording have been adapted to the flow of the story for your sake, without compromising the integrity of what happened and is still happening.

We beg your indulgence if you played a part in this experience but your name or your role isn't mentioned. The whole telling would take many more pages than this book can hold.

And if your life story includes CTE, TBI, or ambiguous loss of any kind, please know that your experience is honored here, even if the details read differently.

Creating Your Own
Ambiguous Loss Ritual or Ceremony

Social rituals are containers of values and are ceremonies that help us through tough transitions. . . . [They] remind us and those around us that a transition (with its gains and losses) has taken place. At the same time, rituals create a social space for unrestrained (but culturally informed) expression of emotions and for active connection with our personal social network that enhances social support and resonates with joys, appeases pains, shares hopes, and mourns the truncation of dreams.

PAULINE BOSS, *Loss, Trauma, and Resilience: Therapeutic Work with Ambiguous Loss*

SIX YEARS TO THE DAY after Zach's first injury, it seemed fitting for us to provide a time and space to publicly and corporately remember, acknowledge, and mourn the very real losses associated with Zach's two traumatic brain injuries. To focus only on the hopeful and positive side had marginalized too much of the emotional reality of the experience. We'd both become convinced of the importance of an event to collectively remember and process our grief. (See chapter 17 for a description of our ceremony of ambiguous loss.)

Whether you consider it a ceremony, an event, a tribute, or a ritual, you and your family may want to custom-design your own with elements that make it significant for you and your guests. Here are guidelines that helped us create our ambiguous loss and celebration ceremonies to make them meaningful for our family and friends.

What is its purpose? To mourn in community? To acknowledge the loss or losses? To celebrate the life that remains?

> What do you and your family need from the event?
> Clearly articulate the purpose of the ceremony to others.

Whom will you invite and why? With whom do you want to grieve? Who are the people likely experiencing this loss with you, even though they may not be aware of it?

Consider the logistics:

Date

Time

Location

Budget

How do you envision the event? Casual or more structured?

Will you provide time for people to reflect? If so, how?

Will anyone speak? Others in attendance may feel the need to say something as they process—perhaps for the first time—their own grief over what they've lost.

You may choose to provide a means for attendees to leave messages you can read later.

Will those attending be involved in any other way?

Will you make use of the arts (video, music, etc.)? Are there pictures, stories, songs, or artifacts that can be woven into the event to help people connect with and lament the losses?

Will you have a handout as a keepsake of the event?

Do you need people to handle specific tasks?

Caterer or food coordinator?

Tech person to run sound or videos?

Photographer?

Videographer?

Parking attendant?

Set-up and tear-down crew?

How can you delegate tasks to those who offer to help?

Day of the ceremony:

Give yourself plenty of time to prepare so you are not rushed.

Find a trusted friend who can coordinate setting up or problem solving at the venue so you can be present with family and friends.

As a courtesy, provide tissues not only for yourself but for others.

Learning to Live with Ambiguous Loss
and to Support Others in Theirs

Thoughts adapted from the McLeods' experiences,
Pauline Boss's works, and biblical teaching

- Take time to find meaning in your ambiguous loss.
  Naming the problem helps, as does remembering
  that the person is here and not here at the same time.
  Research shows that spirituality also helps people find
  meaning in ambiguous loss.

- Recognize that the world is not always just and fair; bad
  things can happen to anyone. Even if we work hard,
  we sometimes won't get what we want in ambiguous
  loss. Self-blame is no help at all, and we can only take
  responsibility for ourselves.

- Negative feelings are normal, as is wondering if it
  would have been easier if the person had died. Talk
  about any guilt you have; guilt is always counter-
  productive when living with ambiguous loss. Talk
  about your conflicted feelings—which are normal—
  in community for support and healing. Tell your story
  and listen to the stories of others. Using the arts will

help you access your emotions. List what you lost but also what you still have.

- In ambiguous loss, though you will never lose the bond of love you had with the person, you have to revise the way you relate to him or her. Don't deny the loss, but don't totally disconnect from the person either. Get all the support you can from family, friends, and those who have been through a similar experience. When you sense it's time for an ambiguous loss ceremony, get help designing the ceremony or rituals that are meaningful to you.

- Realize that ambiguous loss brings unexpected and unwanted change—to habits and routines, traditions, daily life, and relationships. It affects not only your relationship to the person who is in some ways missing, but all relationships within your circle and the missing person's circle of family and friends.

- Because of the ambiguity, the people you care about most will often approach the loss differently. Some will attempt to relate with the missing person and function in the same roles they have always played, as if nothing has happened. Some may function as if the person is dead. Carefully consider and reframe, if necessary, how you will maintain healthy connections with those whose approach differs from your own.

- Learning to live well with both having and not having the missing person will require reflecting on and even reconsidering your identity and the roles you fill. What has remained the same? What has to change? Who are you now within your family structure? At work? As an individual? What do you need, and what can you give?

- Set appropriate boundaries—especially within these new roles—so you can take care of yourself and help others do the same.

- Maintain realistic hopes. If you hold on to unrealistic hopes too long, you won't be able to focus on what needs to get done in your own life and your other relationships. Grieve and also find new hopes and expectations in community, work against injustice if that's an issue in your situation, and avail yourself of spiritual resources.

- Listen well to others in their ambiguous loss. Give each person permission to grieve, and validate the loss. Listen for a *long, long* time. When the person takes a pause from talking, say, "Tell me more" or "Keep going" or "Is there anything else?" Keep inviting people to talk until they are finished. Don't try to fix them or read your autobiography into their lives. And be very careful not to offer pat answers about God's will in their situation.

Holding On to Your Closest Relationship in Ambiguous Loss

WE STARTED THE BOOK with the epigraph, "In times of crisis, every relationship becomes an at-risk relationship." No matter how strong and stable the bond before a hard hit, keeping it intact won't come naturally during the kinds of upheaval that accompany ambiguous loss. Consider these words of counsel that we discovered in our journey or learned from others who walked beside us.

- Carefully manage expectations. Author Anne Lamott notes, "People say that expectations are resentments under construction."
- Be gentle with each other.
- Accept that you and your partner may rarely experience the commonly acknowledged phases of grief (shock, denial, anger, bargaining, depression, acceptance) at the same time and in the same way.
- Focus on being present for the one you love. Ask for the same courtesy in return.

- Acknowledge and accept that you each have different capacities and vulnerabilities related to living well with what's lost and what's not.
- Acknowledge that "getting over it" is something you will never do, but "moving on" is something you must do.

Notes from Tammy
about Football and CTE

WE MADE A CONSCIOUS DECISION as a couple to watch the movie *Concussion* when it was released, despite already living with the long-term consequences we knew the film addressed.

Seeing the movie unfold on the big screen, learning more about the football community's initial resistance to considering what was happening to players over time, and witnessing the results—larger than life—for so many other families left us feeling undone. Rebroken.

For me, the most compelling connection was not the damaged brains, but the damaged relationships and the cost to the children and spouses, the families, extended families, and friends of the players.

Today, few can deny the growing concern and mounting evidence about the long-term negative effects of football-related head trauma. Before Zach suffered his injury, that conversation hardly existed, except between a small band of research scientists and a few former collegiate and NFL players who began to sound the alarm.

For a variety of reasons, the dialogue reached a tipping

point and moved out of the backwaters into the mainstream of sports media coverage just after Zach's injury in 2008. In recent years it has become a point of discussion during college and NFL games, during sports news on TV and radio, in special segments on talk shows, and in locker rooms across the nation.

We now know that many former football players have lost their ability to process information and succumbed to devastating depression and other brain issues that scientists can trace back to head trauma during their playing years. Recently Boston University's CTE Center reported that they'd diagnosed chronic traumatic encephalopathy in 110 of 111 deceased former NFL players studied, and even in seventeen- and eighteen-year-old high school football players.

CTE can begin early, and it's a terrible disease. I grow physically ill over reports of wives and children of former NFL players who endure the pain of watching people they love suffer from symptoms of CTE.

Wives of NFL players rocked by deep brain trauma from multiple concussions are finding their voices on camera, talking more openly about the long-term effects—including the damage significant brain trauma can do to a marriage and family. Football is a game that exacts a heavy price. Sometimes that price is an impossibly hard hit to a player's future, health, and relationships. And younger brains are especially susceptible to brain injury.

NFL players are currently working with the Concussion Legacy Foundation to support a new parent education initiative—Flag Football Under 14—that pushes for no tackle football until the age of fourteen.

Should sons and daughters be encouraged or allowed to play tackle football at all? In light of what our family experienced, I have my own opinion. But this national discussion isn't over. It's just beginning.

Additional Resources
for Your Own Hard Hits

Books

Boss, Pauline. *Ambiguous Loss: Learning to Live with Unresolved Grief.* Cambridge, MA: Harvard University Press, 1999.

Boss, Pauline. *Loss, Trauma, and Resilience: Therapeutic Work with Ambiguous Loss.* New York: W. W. Norton, 2006.

Cantu, Robert, and Mark Hyman. *Concussions and Our Kids: America's Leading Expert on How to Protect Young Athletes and Keep Sports Safe.* Boston: Mariner Books, 2013.

Lewis, C. S. *A Grief Observed.* New York: HarperCollins, 1961, 1994.

Nowinski, Christopher. *Head Games: The Global Concussion Crisis.* Head Games the Film, LLC, 2014.

Sittser, Jerry L. *A Grace Disguised: How the Soul Grows through Loss.* Grand Rapids, MI: Zondervan, 1995, 2004.

Wolterstorff, Nicholas. *Lament for a Son.* Grand Rapids, MI: Eerdmans, 1987.

Websites

More details on the McLeods' story: www.patandtammymcleod.com and www.zacharymcleod.com

HuffPost articles by Tammy McLeod: www.huffingtonpost.com/author/tammy-mcleod

Concussion Legacy Foundation: www.concussionfoundation.org

Boston University Research CTE Center: www.bu.edu/cte

Vice Sports: https://sports.vice.com/en_us/article/8qp3a4/what-would-jesus-think-about-football

**If you have questions about life, God, or
what it might be like to have a relationship with God,
we recommend this site: www.EveryPerson.com.**

Meeting God in the Midst
of Pain and Loss

FOR US, the most profound experiences of God's presence and nearness occurred in the midst of our tragic and painful loss. Here are some of the practices, resources, and activities through which God met us.

The Bible (especially the Psalms)

Prayer (solitude, silence, stillness, retreats, requests for help)

Reflection (journaling)

Spiritual reading (Jerry L. Sittser, Nicholas Wolterstorff, Henri Nouwen)

Beauty/nature (running or walking, retreats and vacations, beaches, mountains, gardens)

Music (worship songs, hymns, reflective classics)

Art (painting, drawing, sculpture, photography, poetry, songwriting, visits to art shows, galleries, and museums)

Individuals (responding when people take time to ask and listen to how you're doing, receiving help from others)

Limits (tempering the desire to master or control, setting boundaries, practicing self-care)

Tears (lament, reading psalms, praying psalms, journaling about what brings you to tears)

Community (accepting practical help with food, cleaning, and respite care from friends and faith community)

Worship (corporate or individual)

Reading and meditating on the last chapters of the four Gospels: Matthew 26–28; Mark 14–16; Luke 22–24; and John 18–21.

Recognizing that we are praying to a crucified God— a God who endured suffering, pain, and death to save us from it.

Being honest with God in prayer. Laying our wants before Him. Although we may not receive everything we ask for, we receive peace as we bring these longings to a God who understands our grief.

Resting in Scriptures
for Times of Loss

I love you, LORD, my strength.
The LORD is my rock, my fortress and my deliverer;
  my God is my rock, in whom I take refuge. . . .
In my distress I called to the LORD;
  I cried to my God for help.
From his temple he heard my voice;
  my cry came before him, into his ears. . . .
He reached down from on high and took
    hold of me;
  he drew me out of deep waters. . . .
You, LORD, keep my lamp burning;
  my God turns my darkness into light.

PSALM 18:1-2, 6, 16, 28

Blessed are those whose strength is in you,
  whose hearts are set on pilgrimage.
As they pass through the Valley of Baka [tears],
    they make it a place of springs;
  the autumn rains also cover it with pools.

They go from strength to strength,
    till each appears before God in Zion.

PSALM 84:5-7

Satisfy us each morning with your unfailing love,
    so we may sing for joy to the end of our lives.
Give us gladness in proportion to our former misery!
    Replace the evil years with good.

PSALM 90:14-15, NLT

Whoever dwells in the shelter of the Most High
    will rest in the shadow of the Almighty.
I will say of the LORD, "He is my refuge and
      my fortress,
    my God, in whom I trust."

PSALM 91:1-2

When I said, "My foot is slipping,"
    your unfailing love, LORD, supported me.
When anxiety was great within me,
    your consolation brought me joy.

PSALM 94:18-19

He will listen to the prayers of the destitute.
    He will not reject their pleas.

PSALM 102:17, NLT

They cried to the LORD in their trouble,
    and he saved them from their distress.
He sent out his word and healed them;

he rescued them from the grave.
Let them give thanks to the LORD for his unfailing love
    and his wonderful deeds for mankind. . . .
Let the one who is wise heed these things
    and ponder the loving deeds of the LORD.

PSALM 107:19-21, 43

The cords of death entangled me,
    the anguish of the grave came over me;
    I was overcome by distress and sorrow.
Then I called on the name of the LORD:
    "LORD, save me!"
The LORD is gracious and righteous;
    our God is full of compassion.
The LORD protects the unwary;
    when I was brought low, he saved me.
Return to your rest, my soul,
    for the LORD has been good to you.
For you, LORD, have delivered me from death,
    my eyes from tears,
    my feet from stumbling,
that I may walk before the LORD
    in the land of the living.

PSALM 116:3-9

When hard pressed, I cried to the LORD;
    he brought me into a spacious place.
The LORD is with me; I will not be afraid.
    What can mere mortals do to me?
The LORD is with me; he is my helper. . . .

The LORD is my strength and my defense;
    he has become my salvation.

PSALM 118:5-7, 14

Since we are surrounded by such a huge crowd of
witnesses to the life of faith, let us strip off every weight
that slows us down, especially the sin that so easily trips
us up. And let us run with endurance the race God has
set before us. We do this by keeping our eyes on Jesus,
the champion who initiates and perfects our faith.
Because of the joy awaiting him, he endured the cross,
disregarding its shame. Now he is seated in the place of
honor beside God's throne. Think of all . . . he endured
. . . then you won't become weary and give up.

HEBREWS 12:1-3, NLT

Endnotes

CHAPTER 2

20   *"You give and take away"*: Matt Redman, Beth Redman, "Blessed Be Your Name," copyright © 2002 Thankyou Music, Capitol CMG Publishing.

CHAPTER 3

33   *"Behold, I am doing a new thing"*: Isaiah 43:19, ESV

CHAPTER 5

53   *"Everlasting, Your light"*: Joel Houston, "From the Inside Out," copyright © 2005 Hillsong Music Publishing (APRA) (adm. in the US and Canada at CapitolCMGPublishing.com). All rights reserved. Used by permission.

56   *"Beauty in Suffering" lyrics:* Tammy McLeod, copyright © 2010.

CHAPTER 8

94   *"Something is over"*: Nicholas Wolterstorff, *Lament for a Son* (Grand Rapids, MI: Eerdmans, 1987), 46–47.

CHAPTER 9

107   *"Your will above all else"*: Joel Houston, "From the Inside Out," copyright © 2005 Hillsong Music Publishing (APRA) (adm. in the US and Canada at CapitolCMGPublishing.com). All rights reserved. Used by permission.

CHAPTER 10

113   *"It is well"*: Horatio Spafford, "It Is Well with My Soul," words written in 1873.

CHAPTER 13

154   *"It still was a good day"*: Aimee Herd, "In Defeat, Glory to God Shines Brighter in Tebow," *Breaking Christian News*, January 17, 2012, http://www.breakingchristiannews.com/articles/display_art.html?ID=9736.

CHAPTER 15

175 *"There is no disease":* M. K. Blanchard, "Be Ye Glad," © Gotz Music, Benson.

CHAPTER 16

182 *two types of ambiguous loss:* Pauline Boss, "Ambiguous Loss," Pauline Boss, http://www.ambiguousloss.com/about/faq.

183 *"Closely attached people":* Pauline Boss, *Loss, Trauma, and Resilience: Therapeutic Work with Ambiguous Loss.* (New York: W. W. Norton and Company, 2006), 162.

183 *"learn how to hold two opposing":* Boss, *Loss, Trauma, and Resilience*, 16.

184 *"the maintaining of two or more logically incompatible":* Webster's Third New International Unabridged Dictionary (1961), s.v. "ambiguity."

184 *"is the most stressful loss":* Pauline Boss, *Ambiguous Loss: Learning to Live with Unresolved Grief* (Cambridge, MA: Harvard University Press, 1999), 20, emphasis added.

185 *I would need to "temper":* Boss, *Loss, Trauma, and Resilience*, 99.

189 *the devastation caused by unresolved grief:* Boss, *Ambiguous Loss*, 59.

189 *"families of the physically":* Boss, *Loss, Trauma, and Resilience*, 19.

CHAPTER 17

200 *"Today we pray for Zach":* Ron Sanders, "Litany of Ambiguous Loss," copyright © 2014 by Ron Sanders. Used with permission.

CHAPTER 18

209 *"We don't just each have a gap":* Nicholas Wolterstorff, *Lament for a Son* (Grand Rapids, MI: Eerdmans, 1987), 99.

210 *"I did not get over the loss":* Jerry L. Sittser, *A Grace Disguised: How the Soul Grows through Loss* (Grand Rapids, MI: Zondervan, 2004), 45–46.

CHAPTER 19

216 *"a presence and a safe space":* Henri Nouwen, *Adam: God's Beloved* (Maryknoll, NY: Orbis Books, 1997), 64.

219 *"The experience of loss":* Jerry L. Sittser, *A Grace Disguised: How the Soul Grows through Loss* (Grand Rapids, MI: Zondervan, 2004), 146.

CREATING YOUR OWN AMBIGUOUS LOSS RITUAL OR CEREMONY

241 *"Social rituals are containers":* Pauline Boss, *Loss, Trauma, and Resilience: Therapeutic Work with Ambiguous Loss* (New York: W. W. Norton and Company, 2006), xiv.

HOLDING ON TO YOUR CLOSEST RELATIONSHIP IN AMBIGUOUS LOSS

249 *"People say that expectations"*: Anne Lamott, *Hallelujah Anyway: Rediscovering Mercy* (New York: Penguin, 2017), 80.

249 *phases of grief:* The stages of grief were first introduced by Elisabeth Kübler-Ross in her book *On Death and Dying* (New York: Simon & Schuster, reprint edition 2011). Though *shock* wasn't included in her original list, it's often acknowledged as an initial stage now.

NOTES FROM TAMMY ABOUT FOOTBALL AND CTE

251 *the movie* Concussion: To read more of my reflections on this film, see my article "Beyond the Field: Dealing with Ambiguous Loss," *HuffPost*, December 6, 2017, www.huffingtonpost.com/entry/beyond-the-field -dealing_b_9144312.html.

252 *110 of 111 deceased former NFL players:* Boston University School of Medicine, "New Study of 111 Deceased Former NFL Players Finds 99 Percent Had CTE," July 25, 2017, https://www.bumc.bu.edu/busm /2017/07/25/new-study-of-111-deceased-former-nfl-players-finds-99 -percent-had-cte/.

252 *even in . . . high school football players:* A. J. Perez, "New Boston University Study Links Repetitive Hits to Head, not Concussions, to CTE," *USA Today*, January 18, 2018.

252 *NFL players are currently working:* For more information, see https:// concussionfoundation.org/programs/flag-football/testimonials.

About the Authors

Pat McLeod serves as a Harvard Chaplain for Cru, an inter-denominational Christian ministry. He grew up in Wyoming and played football at Montana State University. Pat holds an MA in Theological Studies from the International School of Theology, and an MA in Science and Religion and a PhD in Practical Theology from Boston University.

Pat created and helped teach an award-winning philosophy course in Science and Religion at Montana State University. He and Tammy are founding members of the Mamelodi Initiative—a mentoring and educational program aimed at helping youth in South Africa learn, grow, dream, and achieve.

Tammy McLeod, a Harvard Chaplain for Cru and the Director of College Ministry for Park Street Church in Boston, often speaks, teaches, and writes on spiritual formation, prayer, and ambiguous loss. Tammy and Pat have helped launch and lead campus ministries in California, Japan, Montana, Russia, and Boston, and are certified instructors for Interpersonal Communications, Inc. Tammy is also a singer-songwriter and writes for the *Huffington Post*. She received her MA in Spiritual Formation from Gordon-Conwell Theological Seminary.

Zach and Pat with Cynthia

CYNTHIA RUCHTI is a speaker and author of more than two dozen books. She tells stories hemmed-in-Hope through novels, nonfiction, and devotionals, and she has served as a contributing writer for two Bible projects. For thirty-three years, Cynthia wrote and produced a daily radio broadcast—*The Heartbeat of the Home*, which aired on forty-eight stations across the country. Cynthia is a founding member of Deliver Hope—a ministry to at-risk youth. She now serves as a literary agent with Books & Such Literary Management.